"I know no one who is leveraging her everyday life more for the glory of God than Gloria Furman. I want to learn about God and grace from people who live it and fight to do so. I've seen my friend do both beautifully. Gloria has taken the bigness of God and laid him into the cracks of the mundane, and somehow the mundane starts to feel big."

Jennie Allen, author, *Stuck: The Places We Get Stuck and the God Who Sets Us Free*

"This is sustaining grace, this is the desired haven: to know his steadfast love that saves and keeps us. *Glimpses of Grace* is not a how-to. It is a true friend's invitation to see and know the Lord's steadfast love displayed in every wave, big and small. Gloria offers encouragement rooted in her personal experience and wisdom from saints who have weathered the storms decades and even centuries before us. May you catch glimpses of the Lord's steadfast love and find an anchor for your soul."

Lauren Chandler, writer; speaker; singer; wife of Matt Chandler, The Village Church, Flower Mound, Texas

"Gloria is real! She's going to tell you about the smell of her kitchen floor and the steadfast love of her Savior. Jonathan Edwards is right in there with peanut butter sandwiches and sprinkles. The grace this book shows us is no vague idea; it's the biblical gospel infusing the stuff of life—the daily life of a homemaker. Strongly, humbly, and winsomely, this book calls homemakers (and all of us) to walk in faith, connecting the visible with the invisible."

Kathleen B. Nielson, Director of Women's Initiatives, The Gospel Coalition

"*Glimpses of Grace* is a beautiful picture of what it looks like to see Jesus Christ every day in every circumstance. Our friend Gloria takes the glories of Christ's life and opens our eyes to their realities in the seemingly mundane circumstances of our lives. She builds a longing to know more of God and to believe that he is present in all of our work as mothers and wives. Her passion for missions and joy in God is contagious. We are excited to recommend this book to anybody wanting to see the ultimate reality of satisfaction in Christ alone for every day of your life."

Elyse Fitzpatrick and Jessica Thompson, authors, *Give Them Grace*

D0176696

"We need gospel fuel to joyfully serve our families, and that's what *Glimpses of Grace* provides. Many days I unload a barrage of law upon my family, when what they need from me is grace, encouragement, and reminders of God's faithfulness. I thank the Lord for using Gloria to point me to the glorious gospel of his grace so that I might extend the same grace to my husband and children. As homemakers we can be smothered by the ordinary, blinded by the mundane, living in a fog of routine and fatigue, unable to see how to clean messy noses or break up sibling squabbles for the glory of God. In *Glimpses of Grace* Gloria helps to lift the fog by showing us how the gospel can change our perspective as we serve and love our families."

Kristie Anyabwile, homemaker; mom; wife of
Thabiti Anyabwile, First Baptist Church of Grand Cayman

"Every homemaker, every mother, every woman, has experienced the disconnect between what she knows and what she feels, between knowing that what she is doing is good and the reality that it is exasperating and seems unfulfilling. In *Glimpses of Grace* Gloria Furman brings the gospel to bear on a woman's distinct calling. With precision and grace she shows that the good news of all that Jesus Christ accomplished, when properly understood and carefully applied, will transform the way a woman carries out the task the Lord has given her."

Aileen Challies and Tim Challies, author, *The Discipline of Spiritual Discernment*; blogger, challies.com

Glimpses of Grace

Glimpses of Grace

Treasuring the Gospel in Your Home

GLORIA FURMAN

Foreword by Lauren Chandler

WHEATON, ILLINOIS

Glimpses of Grace: Treasuring the Gospel in Your Home

Copyright © 2013 by Gloria C. Furman

Published by Crossway
              1300 Crescent Street
              Wheaton, Illinois 60187

Cover design: Crystal Courtney

First printing 2013

Printed in the United States of America

Scripture quotations are from the ESV® Bible (The Holy Bible, English Standard Version®), copyright © 2001 by Crossway. 2011 Text Edition. Used by permission. All rights reserved.

All emphases in Scripture quotations have been added by the author.

Trade paperback ISBN: 978-1-4335-3605-2
PDF ISBN: 978-1-4335-3606-9
Mobipocket ISBN: 978-1-4335-3607-6
ePub ISBN: 978-1-4335-3608-3

Library of Congress Cataloging-in-Publication Data

Furman, Gloria, 1980-
   Glimpses of grace : treasuring the gospel in your home /
Gloria Furman ; foreword by Lauren Chandler.
      pages   cm
   Includes bibliographical references and index.
   ISBN 978-1-4335-3605-2
   1. Grace (Theology) 2. Families—Religious life.
3. Home—Religious aspects—Christianity. I. Title.
BT761.3.F87   2013
248.4—dc23   2012050930

Crossway is a publishing ministry of Good News Publishers.

VP		25	24	23	22	21	20	19	18	17	16
16	15	14	13	12	11	10	9	8	7	6	

To David,
who tenderly reminds me every mundane day,
"This is the day that the LORD has made;
let us rejoice and be glad in it."
Psalm 118:24

Contents

Foreword

When you're drowning, the last thing you need is a tutorial on five easy steps to swim like a fish. What you need, what you're utterly desperate for, is something that will keep you afloat. Something that you can grab onto and not let go. Something that doesn't need you to sustain it, but rather something that can bear the full weight of your desperation.

Overwhelming waves and deep waters can come in every shape and depth imaginable: a newborn baby, the loss of a job, a chronic illness, a move, a change in a friendship, terminal cancer, a wrestle with your faith, the death of a loved one, a new chapter of parenting, a season of singleness beyond what you'd imagined, more responsibility heaped on a plate already a mile high and even the bleak prospect of what seems to be decades of the mundane—endless loads of laundry, dirty dishes, dust-bunnied floors, and leaky faucet noses. All the places in which you feel in over your head.

Our human tendency is to ask, what steps do I need to take either to make this work or to make this go away? The proof is in the pages—web pages on how to make one's self marketable (to a lifeless job market or to the dating people market). Books of pages line shelves in the local bookstore on what to eat to beat cancer, how to grieve a loss, how to make good kids, how to grow your own garden, raise your own chickens, sew your own clothes, feather your nest with flea market finds refurbished (by you, thanks to

Pinterest), homeschool your kids, create a blog about it, and still have dinner steaming on the table when your husband gets home.

We do well to seek advice. This is wisdom. But there's something to being at your wits' end that begs for more than instruction. Psalm 107 illustrates a season in the storm. Men in ships doing business on great waters are literally struck by a tempest. Scripture says, "They reeled and staggered like drunken men and were at their wits' end" (v. 27). Their response to being completely helpless was to cry out to the Lord. No how-tos, no cute preservers, but just an honest and urgent plea to be delivered from a situation that was more than they could navigate. What did the Lord do on their behalf? He showed them his steadfast love. He calmed the waters, hushed the sea, and brought them to their desired haven.

This is sustaining grace, this is the desired haven: to know his steadfast love that saves and keeps us. *Glimpses of Grace* is not a how-to. It is a true friend's invitation to see and know the Lord's steadfast love displayed in every wave, big and small. Gloria offers encouragement rooted in her personal experience and wisdom from saints who have weathered the storms decades and even centuries before us. May you catch glimpses of his steadfast love and find an anchor for your soul.

Lauren Chandler

Acknowledgments

Aliza, Norah, and *Judson,* this book would be quite dull and would have fewer pages without your precious personalities.

I'm thankful for the encouragement from the online community at the *Domestic Kingdom blog* and from *Collin Hansen* and *Tony Reinke.* I'm also grateful that my catalyzing friend *Jennie Allen* convinced me to try writing something longer than a blog post. A huge thank you goes to *Justin Taylor* and *Lydia Brownback* and the people at *Crossway.*

My brothers and sisters in Christ at *Redeemer Church of Dubai* prayed for me and sweet sisters gave me their time and practical help so I could work on this book: *Sarah Wilson, Sarah Lawrence, Laura Davies,* and *Kanta Marchandani. Don and Becky,* thank you for hosting my talkative baby and me for two writing retreats and for not being frustrated that I left coffee cups all over your house and goldfish crackers under the bed.

When *Kevin and Katie Cawley* selflessly gave me their copy of Milton Vincent's *A Gospel Primer for Christians* right off of their coffee table, I had no idea just how true their bold recommendation would be. That book really did change my life. *Samantha Muthiah,* thank you for getting me a copy of Staci Eastin's *The Organized Heart* and for all the subsequent conversations about gospel centrality that followed.

Jeremiah Burroughs and *Richard Sibbes* left a legacy of hope in the resurrection that has served to spur me on to live in the light that overwhelmed the grave. It's also hard to quantify the impact that the ministries of *John Piper, D. A. Carson*, and *Paul Tripp* have had on me.

A constant encourager for this work from start to finish was *my husband, Dave*. He knew how much I needed to write for the good of my own soul and he made sacrifices to make it happen. Thank you!

Introduction

In the first draft of this introduction I wrote, "I want to flesh out the practical implications of the gospel in everyday life."

Then the thought occurred to me that I have never "fleshed out" anything before. I've only ever *de*-fleshed things—like rotisserie chickens and Thanksgiving turkeys.

The other metaphors I was reaching for weren't working, either. I blamed the writer's block on my mommy brain. Then it hit me.

Introductions are like the "why" question, which is a question that I answer all day long.

Funny enough, today's big "why" dialogue was about cooking chicken. I have two daughters of preschool age, and they were watching me make chicken nuggets and boil pasta. One of them declared, "I want to cook, too. Give me the knife, Mommy!" She's not even five years old; she cannot be trusted to wield a knife.

I began to reason with her, "You aren't responsible enough to handle this big knife."

Why? (Here we go.)

"Because it's a heavy, sharp knife and it's dangerous. You could cut yourself."

Why? "Because you're so little and small, and only big adults can handle knives like this."

All right, then I'll boil the noodles. "I don't want you to touch the stove top, either."

Why? "Because you aren't mature enough to use the gas and lighter properly."

Why? "Because they're very tricky to work, even for Mommy."

But I can do tricky things. I can unclip my car seat and I can count to one hundred—when you help me. "Sorry, Kiddo, you're still not qualified to cook with fire yet."

Why? [Sigh.]

This dialogue makes sense when you're talking to a preschooler about the dangers in a kitchen. But sometimes we think of theology in this way. We think it's too dangerous, too tricky, and we don't feel confident that we're qualified to handle it. We feel we should leave the work of theology to professors, pastors, and Sunday school teachers.

Besides, what does theology have to do with homemaking and things that everybody does, regardless of their faith?

Even despite our reservations and suppositions, all of us handle theology every day. We can't help but theologize! The fact that everybody does mundane things, regardless of their religion, is another reason that we ought to consider what makes the way we live distinctly Christian.

We live in God's world, we're made in God's image, and we interact with other people who have eternal souls. That makes theology vastly important and immensely life changing in our everyday mundane.

Theology is for homemakers who need to know who God is, who they are, and what this mundane life is all about.

That's why I wrote this book.

As homemakers who are made in God's image and desire to live for God, we need to know what God's intentions are for us and for the work we do in the home.

More specifically, we need to know: What does the gospel have to do with our everyday lives in the home? How does the gospel impact our dish washing, floor mopping, bill paying, friend making, guest hosting, and dinner cooking?

How does the fact that Jesus himself bore our sins in his body on the tree so that we might die to sin and live to righteousness (1 Pet. 2:24) make a difference in my mundane life today?

Where do we get our spiritual direction from? Should we follow our hearts or trust our guts? Do whatever best-selling books at the moment contain the secret to the good life? Is the answer to simply live in the moment, stopping to smell the fabric softener every once in awhile?

There are a lot of half-baked spiritual ideas that masquerade as Christian theology. How can we tell the difference? This book is not so much a critique of these philosophies but a description of the distinctly Christian hope of God's glory and how it relates to the home.

God's Word, the Bible, says that we were created for God to live for God's glory. With all that is in me, that's what I want for my life. I know the "created for him" part is already done (since I'm already alive). The part that's left—*living for him*—that's what I need help with. This morning, this afternoon, this evening, and in the middle of the night when I'm up with the baby, I want to know how I am a partaker of God's promises in Christ through the gospel (Eph. 3:6).

Ordinary life in my home is often far from boring. Life is hectic and peaceful, joyful and painful. Life in the home can be all of these things because that's where *life* happens.

We're a motley crew of sinners made in God's image who are trying to live alongside each other under the gospel of God's grace. It's both beautiful and messy. So how does the "living hope through the resurrection of Jesus Christ from the dead" (1 Pet. 1:3) change the way I live my life?

The biggest questions I want to explore in this book are these: *What does the gospel have to do with our lives in the home? How does this grace change the way we live?*

Today Is Monday

Probably the one thing I was most excited about when I began writing this book was the accountability to be disciplined to think about these questions every day. What a joy!

And the only thing better than writing about how to treasure the gospel in your home is eating pretzels dipped in leftover vanilla frosting while you're writing. Now I have about a gram of salt rattling around in my keyboard!

Glimpses of Grace is about how we live in the "already but not yet" time in God's redemptive history. Jesus is alive—he is not in the grave. The triumph of Easter Sunday is the reality in which we live every moment of every day. The things in our home have the potential to propel us to revel in the reality of Easter. Our homes also have the potential to distract us as we fix our hearts not on what is unseen but on what we see—the larger-than-life dishes piled high in the sink.

In this book I want to talk about what a treasure the gospel is to us, especially in our homes, propelling us to exult in the hope of God's glory. Because God is good, we have an infinite number of reasons to praise him in our homes. "Oh give thanks to the LORD, for he is good; for his steadfast love endures forever!" (1 Chron. 16:34).

I realize this is a huge topic to discuss because it impacts our lives every day and has implications for eternity. I also realize that today is Monday, and the buzzer on the dryer just went off, and you've got to get your clothes out before they wrinkle. On your way to the laundry room you might notice a suspicious trail of fluid leading to the bathroom where you can hear your recently potty-trained child sniffling as she tries to hold back humiliated tears. Then the doorbell might ring, and the ringing might remind you that you ignored the alarm for an appointment you're about to be late for.

I totally understand that, because that's where I live, too.

That's why I need to explore how the gospel is the predominant, defining reality in my life.

Remembering to live in God's grace as I live in my home isn't easy for me, and that's why I need to process through the content of this book over and over again. Augustine said what my heart feels: "I count myself one of the number of those who write as they learn and learn as they write."[1]

I'm eager to know the "how" of how God intends to finish the good work he has started in me as he conforms me to the image of his Son Jesus (Phil. 1:6). I desperately want to glorify him in whatever I do (1 Cor. 10:31). I want to be holy in all my conduct, since it is written, "You shall be holy, for I am holy" (1 Pet. 1:15–16). I want to be an imitator of God, as his beloved child, walking in love as Christ loved me and gave himself up for me (Eph. 5:1–2).

I want to live in the reality that I have been brought to God through his Son. "For Christ also suffered once for sins, the righteous for the unrighteous, that he might bring us to God, being put to death in the flesh but made alive in the spirit" (1 Pet. 3:18).

A Bucket of Ice Water for a Sleepy Soul

I used to believe that this journey of sanctification—the adventure of God working in me, both to will and to work for his good pleasure (Phil. 2:13)—would only be accomplished when I am free from the "distractions" of my life.

As a result of my faulty thinking, I saw my roles as wife, mother, homemaker, and even minister of the gospel as things that detracted, or took away from, my spiritual life. That perspective ruled my day-to-day activities. For example, if I set my alarm clock to attempt to wake up before one of my babies and had my plans foiled, then I would think, "Well, there goes my communion with God today! Thanks a lot, _____!"

Part of my wake-up call was when we added more children to our family. My anxiety over trying to "get some time with God" got worse, and suddenly I realized that my prayer life had plummeted into near nonexistence. Tim Keller's comment on prayer was a bucket of ice water over my sleepy soul: "Your private prayer life is one of the key indicators that your Christianity is inner and true and not just the product of your environment."

I had allowed my spiritual life to be relegated to an easy chair with a cup of hot coffee in a quiet house without any noise or clutter or *life*. My mind needed to be renewed according to the gospel (Eph. 4:23).

This book is about how we experience the grace of the gospel as we go about our daily lives in the home. It's not about how to transcend to "a happy place" above the reality of life in the home. It's not about how to relish our mundane existence and cherish it as if it were an all-satisfying fountain if we would only soak it in for its own sake.

Glimpses of Grace is about how God's power in the gospel can transform us for his glory as we live by faith—right where we are in the mundane of our homes. It's about how God has made us new in his likeness of true righteousness and holiness (Eph. 4:24). The grace of God in Christ radically changes us. But how does he change the way we wash the same dishes every day? How does the gospel change the way our heart responds when we hear the doorbell ring during supper?

Just Feed Me the Gospel

At unfathomable cost to himself, Jesus died to reconcile us to God. His life and death were not just good examples for us to follow. When we repent of our sins, believing that Christ's death on the cross was for us in our place, God saves us. He forgives us in Christ (Eph. 4:32). He ransoms us "with the precious blood of Christ, like that of a lamb without blemish or spot" (1 Pet. 1:18–19). God justifies us as though we had never sinned as he gives us the righteousness of his perfect Son (Phil. 3:9).

"In him we have redemption through his blood, the forgiveness of our trespasses, according to the riches of his grace, which he lavished upon us, in all wisdom and insight" (Eph. 1:7–8). At no point can we say, "I did it! It was hard work, but I tried my best and I did it." No, it is *God* who saves us, "for by grace you have been saved through faith. And this is not your own doing; it is the gift of God" (Eph. 2:8).

God seals believers in Christ with the indwelling Holy Spirit. And so God begins his ongoing work of sanctification, while the Holy Spirit assures us that we are God's children. Through his work of grace, God changes the dynamics of our hearts so that we long to be with him. God also provides the power we need to be like him.

Apart from knowing God, we have no hope for being a wise parent, spouse, friend, floor sweeper, or bill payer. Because God raised Jesus from the dead and gave him glory, our faith and hope are in God (1 Pet. 1:21), not in our ever-changing circumstances or in the comforts of our homes and meticulously planned routines.

I told my husband as I started writing this book that since this book is about how the gospel applies to life, that means there are infinite numbers of chapters to write. I imagined myself just typing the gospel over and over again to fill up a book-sized gap between two attractive cover pages. And that's what I tried to do, illustrating ideas with personal examples from the home.

There's nothing I can say in this book that the gospel hasn't already said, so I'm just hoping to keep pointing you back to the gospel in every way I possibly can. Rejoicing in God through the gospel is what my soul needs, and I hope your soul benefits from it as well.

I'm glad you're coming along on this adventure with me.

Contained within the gospel are the brilliant manifestations of the character of God—whom we need an eternity to behold and enjoy! We're going to discuss how it is that the God whose "steadfast love is great to the heavens, your faithfulness to the clouds" (Ps. 57:10) is doing a powerful work in your life right under the roof of your own home.

As my wannabe-cook daughter's favorite line from an animated movie about a rat that is a chef goes: "Let's do this thing!"

Part 1

Your Foundation in the Mundane

1

Today's Forecast: Mundane with a 100 Percent Chance of Miraculous

Again. He left his smoothie cup on the counter overnight *again*. My husband, Dave, is a gifted, brilliant man. But sometimes kitchen-related common sense eludes him.

Crusted Blueberries and Being Rude

Now there was no way the crusted blueberry bits were going to come off of this cup without some serious work on my part. I started talking to myself aloud (do you do this too?). "I don't have time for this," I mumbled. I gritted my teeth and set to scrubbing with vigor, and when Dave passed by the kitchen I let out an exasperated sigh and exaggerated my scrubbing efforts. "Gee, I hope I can get this cup clean. You didn't rinse it out."

Dave apologized and said he had simply forgotten.

"How rude," I thought. "He knows how much work I do. The least he could have done was rinse out the cup. Rude . . ." But really, I was the rude one, and I knew it. The Holy Spirit brought to mind the famous love passage in 1 Corinthians 13: "Love is patient and kind; love does not envy or boast; it is not arrogant or rude. It does not insist on its own way; it is not irritable or resentful; it does not rejoice at wrongdoing, but rejoices with the truth. Love bears all things, believes all things, hopes all things, endures all things. Love never ends" (1 Cor. 13:4–8). The New International Version translates verse 8 as "love never fails."

I knew I had failed to show love. Again. I fail at this every day. What hope is there for me to sacrificially give my life away as Jesus did, when I can't even love others by doing something so menial like washing dishes? My only hope must be in the God who is "merciful and gracious, slow to anger, and abounding in steadfast love and faithfulness" (Ex. 34:6).

Does God Rule Your Mundane?

This is such a stereotypical example of my life. I'm the wife of a busy church planter and mother to three kids, four years old and under. We live in the Middle East where sand seeps into every crack in the windows and doors and leaves a gritty film all over the floor for me to sweep. I do eight loads of laundry and clip four sets of fingernails and toenails each week.

My life is all things ordinary.

That's why I loved writing this book. I need this message of grace and hope every single day. That's because sometimes I launch into full-blown pity parties like the one you just read about. I used to think this sour kind of attitude about homemaking was necessary, acceptable, and even a rite of passage. After all, a common encouragement to someone in the midst of the trenches in homemaking or raising children is to console them with thoughts of "this, too, shall pass." We "grin and bear it" and talk about everything we're going to do "someday" when we "get our real life back."

Those colloquial phrases used to be the summation of my hope. I believed that if I could just get through this awful and seemingly interminable season, then I would come out on the other side bruised and worn down; but at least it would be over. Perhaps then I would be free to serve the Lord with gladness, and I would be content.

But I was wrong.

When I attended a marriage conference taught by Paul Tripp,

he said something that devastated me. Tripp said, "If God doesn't rule your mundane, then he doesn't rule you. Because that's where you live." Dramatic, life-altering moments come only a few times during our lifetime—that's why they're dramatic. The rest of our lives are lived in the common, ordinary mundane.

Home managing is my ordinary. Regardless of what your normal is, I'm sure we can agree that that's where we live.

Glorify God in Whatever You Do

I know that serving my family is akin to serving Jesus, and when I manage my home I should work as unto the Lord. Colossians 3:23–24 says, "Whatever you do, work heartily, as for the Lord and not for men, knowing that from the Lord you will receive the inheritance as your reward. You are serving the Lord Christ."

We ought to consider our home managing "as the creation of a living organism that nurtures the peace of Christ and the righteousness of God."[1] Statements like that one encouraged me greatly.

I already believed Scripture, as it extols the role of a homemaker as worth tremendous value. I had no problem seeing homemaking as meaningful in light of eternity. Eternal perspective? Got it. But what about *today*? How is today included in the scope of eternity? Tripp's comment reminded me that the Bible has a lot to say about the mundane. First Corinthians 10:31 says, "So, whether you eat or drink, or whatever you do, do all to the glory of God."

Yes! *Of course* I want to glorify God! He is the supreme treasure of the universe, and he is worthy of my everything. At the core of my being, my greatest desire it to bring glory to God. I've even considered stenciling the Westminster Catechism on my wall to remind me of this truth:

Question 1:   What is the chief end of man?
Answer: Man's chief end is to glorify God and to enjoy Him forever.[2]

Whether I ought to make my goal glorifying God in everything was not in question. I knew that living for his glory is to be my greatest joy. My problem was simply *how?* How can I fold laundry and settle sibling squabbles to God's glory when I am so prone to failure because of my sin? *How* does the gospel make me into a woman who scrubs toilets or wipes runny noses heartily as for the Lord? *How* does the gospel make me into a woman who cares about honoring God in the way I fold laundry and serve dinner?

How does my citizenship in heaven (Phil. 3:20) change how I manage my home?

Diapers Can Set Your Heart and Mind on Things Above

If the Word of God is for everyday people who do everyday things, then surely Scripture talks about how we can magnify God in the midst of the mundane. And if the mundane moments of dishes and diapers can be done with an aim to enjoying God, then the spiritual vitality we will experience in our home is nothing short of miraculous.

The opportunity for growth in holiness lies right in front of your face—sitting in the tepid dishwasher, festering in the laundry basket, at your crowded dinner table, and under the car seat where your toddler stashed her leftover granola bar for later. Sure, fuzzy mold might be growing there, but in these moments it is also where growth in holiness happens.

Right where we are, we can see glimpses of grace as we learn to apply passages like Colossians 3:1–3, which says, "If then you have been raised with Christ, seek the things that are above, where Christ is, seated at the right hand of God. Set your minds on things that are above, not on things that are on earth. For you have died, and your life is hidden with Christ in God."

God powerfully brings our ministry to fruition and our deeds done in faith (2 Thess. 1:11). So, that umpteenth dirty diaper, when viewed in light of the hope and promises in God's Word, can be a significant means of God's transforming work in your life.

The Cross, the Crown, and the "Titus 2 Woman"

Let's look at Titus 2 as an example. Titus 2 is a nitty-gritty, practical, how-to list of qualities that godly women ought to have and things godly women ought to do. Women are to be reverent in behavior, not slanderers or enslaved to alcohol (v. 3). Women are to be self-controlled, pure, working at home, kind, and submissive to their husband (v. 5). Women are to teach what is good (i.e., "sound doctrine," v. 1), training younger women to love their husband and children (v. 4).

Titus 2 contains not only a to-do list of things that you could post on an index card on your bathroom mirror. Titus 2 also gives us our motive for doing these things, which is that "the word of God may not be reviled" (v. 5) and that "in everything they may adorn the doctrine of God our Savior" (v. 10). Motivation can't be written on an index card—it must be written on your heart.

How does this motive to adorn the gospel of God get written on our hearts? Our hearts must be transformed by Christ. Verse 11 says, "For the grace of God has appeared, bringing salvation for all people." Paul adds in verse 12 that this grace is "training us to renounce ungodliness and worldly passions, and to live self-controlled, upright, and godly lives in the present age."

The gospel motivation is presented with a promise of a future hope. As we are doing these things, we are "waiting for our blessed hope, the appearing of the glory of our great God and Savior Jesus Christ, who gave himself for us to redeem us from all lawlessness and to purify for himself a people for his own possession who are zealous for good works" (vv. 13–14).

That's where faith comes in and the rubber meets the road. When I look back to the cross and see that God did not spare his own Son for me (Rom. 8:32), and when I look forward to God's promises of future glory (Titus 2:13), he gives me the power to graciously pick up after my husband, who forgot to rinse his cup, and not seethe with anger and lash out verbally.

Two Wrong Ways Don't Make It Right

I can imagine what you may be thinking at this point because I'm thinking it too. I believe that is true, but I've got lots of things going against me. I can't hold that idea in my mind long enough to meditate on it. I can already hear static baby noises from the next room coming through the baby monitor. I can't apply these truths with consistency. What if it's not just a dirty cup but an entire house that looks like a sandstorm was unleashed inside? What then?

I need to have my heart change.

If you're like me, then you might be ready to give up right now. That is so tempting for me. I see the high standards of holiness, but I know I can't possibly meet them. In this case I might just slop my way through the dishes, grumbling in my heart and making snide remarks about "how many times have I reminded you" hoping to shame my husband into making a sincere confession of how he's wrong and I'm right. (When has that strategy ever worked, by the way?)

Or I could approach this scene a different way. I know the Bible says to do all things without grumbling and to hold onto the gospel instead (Phil. 2:14), and I want to do what is right. God teaches us how to love each other (1 Thess. 4:9). And I want to honor God in everything I do, just as 1 Corinthians 10:31 says I should. I determine that what I need to do is try harder. So I tape an index card with Philippians 2:14 on it to the window above my sink so that I will be reminded not to sin. Then I do the dishes and I hold my tongue as my husband passes by the kitchen. Now I've managed to avoid cutting remarks and clanging the dishes around to solicit attention and a possible apology. Nice work, Gloria, you've done it. I congratulate myself on a job well done. My gloating, however, reveals that I have another problem on my hands: self-righteousness. The forbearance I displayed in the kitchen apparently wasn't a fruit of the Spirit. It was rooted in sinful pride. At the end of the day I'm steeped in self-righteousness

—basking in pride or wallowing in guilt that I could have done a better job.

The dirty dishes are not my biggest problem in life, even though it seems like they are when they're stacked up to the ceiling and I've got a million other things to do. The biggest problem in my life and yours is sin. How can I stand before the God who does all things according to his character, a character that includes perfect justice (2 Thess. 1:6)?

Jesus: A Home Manager's Only Hope

So what can be done? Clearly we can't live our lives lawlessly, taking pot shots at people to make ourselves feel better. And clearly we can't just muster up our self-determination and will power to "do the right thing." I simply can't do it. Either way I choose, I don't please God.

Thankfully there is one who did. Jesus did everything without complaining, including going to the cross to die in my place and taking my sin on himself. Jesus is the ultimate man who lives in sincere submission to God the Father. The Bible teaches that not only is Jesus my example but he is also my Savior. His atoning death did just that—he atoned for (paid for) my sins. And he didn't stay dead. Jesus is the one who says, "I died, and behold I am alive forevermore, and I have the keys of Death and Hades" (Rev. 1:18). When I take hold of Jesus by faith as my only hope to please God, God declares that I am justified. Christ's righteousness becomes mine. That's grace.

The grace shown to me at the cross, and the future grace I look forward to, prevent me from two deadly attitudes:

1) *I'm a terrible housewife.* I know I should do better, and I have no excuses. Why can't I just be like so-and-so who has it all together? I heap on guilt and condemnation and steep myself in pride. Yes, pride. I would rather wallow in introspective self-loathing than repent and look to Christ for acceptance and power to live each moment.

2) *I'm an amazing housewife.* It really is quite remarkable how I can juggle all of these things. My friends say so all the time. I discipline myself to get things done and regardless of what happens, I get it done, and not a hair is out of place while I'm doing it, too. Frankly, I can't understand why so-and-so who has less on her plate can't seem to at least manage what she has. I steep myself in self-righteousness and pride. I would rather bask in my own glory than in the glory of Christ as he gave himself for me on the cross to secure my future.

So grace reminds me to live in the reality of the gospel and the future promised to me. Because of what Christ has already done on my behalf and will do for me in the future, I can reject guilty loathing and prideful gloating.

Milton Vincent put it this way: "The righteousness of God, credited to me through Christ, is not merely something I rest in, but it is also the premier saving reality by which God governs me."[3]

Furthermore, as a result of Christ's work on the cross, I have everything I need for life and godliness (2 Pet. 1:3–4), and all these things are gifts I don't deserve. God is gracious to me "according to his great mercy" (1 Pet. 1:3).

Jesus Died for Me; I Can Trust Him

This grace humbles me. That Jesus would allow himself to be led like a lamb to slaughter and not answer those who reviled him—it takes my breath away. That God would send his Son to die for me and purchase for me "an inheritance that is imperishable, undefiled, and unfading" (1 Pet. 1:4)—I am undone.

The joy of the Lord motivates and strengthens me to give my time to serve others in washing their dishes while looking forward in faith to hear my Savior say to me, "Well done, good and faithful servant." As I joyfully and humbly give my time and energy to do the dirty dishes my husband left behind, I lose nothing and gain everything.

Living in the reality of this gospel and the future promise of glory motivates me to love others as Jesus loves. I have received mercy in Christ Jesus (1 Pet. 2:10). This afternoon at my kitchen sink I must be confident that what he promises for me in the future will come to pass. That's faith.

So here I am at my kitchen sink, scrubbing crusty blueberry bits off the inside of a cup. But instead of grieving over my inadequacies to serve joyfully or gloating with pride that I've restrained my evil tongue from making snide remarks, an entirely different dynamic is at work.

It's faith working through love (Gal. 5:5-6).

God works in me through his Word (1 Thess. 2:13). This gift of grace enables me to praise the Lord and serve others gladly as I confess with tears of joyful relief, "For from him and through him and to him are all things. To him be glory forever. Amen" (Rom. 11:36).

Even in my darkest doubts when I do the same thing again the next day, my hope is still built on the righteousness of Christ. The gospel keeps me relating to God on the basis of Jesus's perfections, not on the illusions of my religious achievements. God strengthens me and protects me according to his faithfulness, not mine (2 Thess. 3:3). So I can scrub dried blueberry bits as unto the Lord as my heart is satisfied in God because his kindness to me in Christ leads me to repentance again and again.

Miraculous in the Mundane

Do you see how everyday life presents opportunities for our growth in holiness? God can use the ordinary moments in your life to glorify himself by conforming you into the image of his Son. That is precisely what he intends to do.

Dirty dishes in the sink or red crayons smushed into an electrical socket by a curious toddler are not just worrisome ordeals in your otherwise uneventful day. They're opportunities to see glimpses of grace.

2

Don't Smurf the Gospel

I can't remember the first time someone shared the gospel with me.

It's not because no one cared to share with me the good news of Jesus. It's because I didn't have ears to hear it. There were many other things I cared about more.

It's possible that I heard the good news of Jesus's death and resurrection hundreds of times over the course of my childhood.

My Story

I was born in a country where religious freedom allowed the Christian message to be broadcast over the radio, advertised on billboards, and discussed freely in the public square. For a period of time I even lived in a section of the country called "The Bible Belt," where there were churches on every corner. My parents faithfully took me to Sunday school, church meetings, and vacation Bible school.

Living in the part of the world where I live now, I realize what a privilege I was given. That my parents brought me to church, celebrated Christian holidays, and talked about Jesus—this was a grace to me that my neighbors here have never known.

I don't have particular memories of all those times I heard the good news of Jesus when I was growing up. Yet I do remember the first time the light of the glory of God in the face of Christ split through the darkness into my heart. And I didn't want to bask in its warmth at first. I wanted to hide. Let me back up this story and tell you how it happened.

Graduating from high school was around the lowest point of my life. The bad choices I had made over the past several years had come to a head, and I acutely felt that I was miserable. Until that point, I had doped myself with the things the world had to offer me to dull the pain of feeling hopeless. I attached my worth and my dreams to solutions that were short-lived and destructive.

I can't decide if the lowest point was earning three traffic tickets driving home from doing something I ought to have been arrested for. Or perhaps it was the persistent feeling I had in my heart that I was trapped in a living hell that I had made for myself. And if I felt like I was in a living hell, you can imagine what my parents must have felt during those very dark years. All the people in my life who shared God's love with me must have felt that their words had been falling on deaf ears.

And yet God is sovereign. I left for university hanging on to a shred of hope.

By God's grace I believed that God exists and that he is personal. I prayed to him and asked for a new life. I didn't know what that meant or how it would happen, but I thought that God was benevolent enough that he would hear if a train wreck like me would ask him for help.

So I packed up the Rubbermaid trunk that my parents bought for me, drove to the residence hall, and said hello to college life. Literally, I said hello to College Life. That was the name of the university ministry of a local church in my college town. The first week I was on campus, I was sitting in the student union waiting in line for something along with some new friends. Another student approached us and asked if we were Christians. I responded affirmatively because I didn't think I was anything else. I was born in a "Christian country" after all, and I did not practice any "foreign" religions. "Christian" was the label I gave myself based on these assumptions and a few others that I'll explain in a minute. One of my friends responded that she was not a Christian.

"No matter!" the girl replied. "Everyone is invited to come to

The Cup tonight for an open-mic night of Christian music! Do you want me to come pick you up from your dorm?"

I still can't believe I was the first one to say yes. I don't know why I said yes. I was and still am a shy person. But nonetheless, I said yes, and two of my friends said they would go, too.

True to her word, Jamie (I asked her name after I told her which dorm we lived in) picked us up in her car and drove us one block over to The Cup. At that event I met lots of people, including a couple of Tiffanys who co-led a freshman Bible study and asked me to join them. I said, "Sure, why not?" Again, I can't believe I said yes.

Then a few months into the semester I started to feel uncomfortable at the Bible study. I couldn't pray for the girl sitting next to me when we shared prayer requests. I didn't take the time to fill out the workbook during the week, because I didn't see the point of the questions. I didn't understand the answers the other girls gave out of their Bibles. And I definitely couldn't relate to the way the Scriptures impacted their everyday lives and deeply *affected* them. I mean, girls would weep or get really excited when they talked about what God meant to them. I began to feel very out of place.

So I expressed my desire to drop out of the study yet remain in the loop with all the social activities, like dinners at IHOP and dancing at Billy Bob's. But I wasn't prepared for the response I was given. It was a question: "Can I suggest that the reason you don't feel comfortable with studying the Bible is because you're not a born-again Christian?"

I thought that was ridiculous, so I listed my spiritual resume in defense. *I am an American. We are all Christian. After all, it says on our money, "In God we trust." I went to Sunday school. I went to church. I went to vacation Bible school. I had Bible verses memorized. Sure, I very much prefer my sin to holiness, but what of it? I'm not nearly as bad a person as so-and-so, and God understands that I am trying my best. So what else is there?*

Praise God, my friend had the courage and mercy to open up her Bible and tell me the truth about my sin.

Midway through that conversation it was apparent that the Word of God had sliced through my stony heart and exposed me for the self-righteous sinner that I was. I thought I could barter my way into God's favor by pointing out my attempts for self-improvement and my relative goodness compared to other people. I came to realize, however, that my sin was against an infinitely holy God. What could I do? God's standard of perfection was impossible. I had no idea who I was dealing with—or rather, who was dealing with me. He was the awesome creator of the universe, who is pure beyond all comprehension.

And I was lost.

Then, by God's grace, I heard the good news, and I believed it.

The good news of Jesus Christ that my friend told me about that day is the news that I want to explicitly clarify in the rest of this chapter. The rest of this book is for unpacking what that means in our everyday lives in the home.

Little Blue People and Christianese

When I was a kid I used to watch the cartoon *The Smurfs*. Smurfs live in a forest and spend their days doing carefree things unless they're trying to avoid the evil wizard who rues their existence. The Smurfs have their own distinct culture marked by normative Smurf behavior and even special vocabulary words. "It's smurfy outside!" "Smurf this for me, will you?" "Find that Smurf!"

Is *Smurf* a noun? An adjective? Not even the Smurfs can put a tiny blue finger on it because of the obscurity of the word.

In this way, the way the Smurfs communicate is not too different from how many of us in the Christian culture do. We have our own rules of acceptable behavior and a unique vocabulary. The pejorative term *Christianese* comes from this phenomenon, where we discuss our faith using words that only other Christians understand. *But do we really understand each other?*

I would hate for you to read this book and not understand a word I'm saying because I'm Smurfy.

Smurfing Around with the Gospel

I wonder if the meaning of the word *gospel* has gone the way of the Smurfs? *Gospel* is one of those words that everyone says but few people define.

In the past week I read a blog post that said, "Adopting a child out of poverty is gospel," heard a testimony where someone said he "believes the gospel," heard a song about "obeying the gospel," read an e-mail about how "the gospel defeats sex trafficking," saw a Facebook status about how someone was excited to "be the gospel," and reviewed a book about ways to "proclaim the gospel." What is "gospel"? Is it a noun? An adjective? A cause? A message? A lifestyle? Is everyone right or at least close to the real meaning of the word?

Clarification and careful definitions are the only way we can know that we rightly understand each other. If we aren't clear on what the Christian gospel is, then what is at stake is not merely a harmless misunderstanding but eternal life and death.

Clarifying the Gospel

Of course, Christians all over the world agree that according to the ancient biblical languages the term *gospel* means "good news." Books are written about the Greek word *euangelion*, the word for *gospel* used in the New Testament. Based on the scopes of the definitions of the word, theologians offer differing perspectives on what gospel means.

Theologians place different emphasis on various dimensions of the gospel (private, personal, cosmic, global), various implications of the gospel (grace for today, hope for tomorrow, peace regarding our past), and its results or fruit (reconciliation with God, redemption of the created order, forgiveness of sins, restored community, escape from judgment and hell, the gift of eternal life).

Things can get pretty smurftastic when people describe the gospel using terms and definitions that may compete with each other. One author may say the gospel is a story you are in, while another says the gospel is the lifestyle you lead. Still others insist the gospel is a historical event or a body of information about Christianity.

I won't try to regurgitate Greek parsing in this chapter or list all the ways the term *gospel* is used today. What I'd like to do in this chapter is to clarify what I believe is an evangelical definition and description of the gospel. Without clarity on the gospel, how will we know how to treasure it in our homes?

I agree with Graeme Goldsworthy's assessment of the smurfy situation: "It cannot be stressed too much that to confuse the gospel with certain important things that go hand in hand with it is to invite theological, hermeneutical and spiritual confusion."[1]

That's a lot to smurf about!

What Is the Gospel?

The gospel is the news of what God has done in Jesus—particularly and supremely in Jesus's death on the cross and resurrection from the dead.

But why did Jesus die? Did he just play his political cards poorly and end up the victim of a jealousy-driven assassination?

Many of my neighbors deny that Jesus died on the cross at all. They say that a substitute hung in his place. If that's true, then Jesus did not die as *our* substitute. Our faith is then worthless, and we are still dead in our sins. Why is it so important that Christians affirm and announce Jesus's death on the cross?

Jesus died to save us from our sins. Here's what I mean when I say that. The Bible says that God is holy and that he created us to worship him. Clearly, the world does not enjoy unhindered worship of the holy creator God. What happened?

God gave a command to the first man and woman he created: "And the LORD God commanded the man, saying, 'You may surely eat of every tree of the garden, but of the tree of the knowledge of good and evil you shall not eat, for in the day that you eat of it you shall surely die'" (Gen. 2:16-17). Satan entered the garden of Eden and tempted Eve to take a bite of the fruit. She did. And then she handed the fruit to her husband, Adam, and he took a bite also.

The apostle Paul explains that the consequences for Adam and Eve's sin of prideful disobedience were cosmic. "Therefore, just as sin came into the world through one man, and death through sin, and so death spread to all men because all sinned" (Rom. 5:12). In a singular act of disobedience against an infinitely holy God, sin and death entered the world. And all of humanity was justly condemned to death.

But this infinitely holy God had mercy. He promised a savior. Listen to the curse God pronounced on Satan: "I will put enmity between you and the woman, and between your offspring and her offspring; he shall bruise your head, and you shall bruise his heel" (Gen. 3:15).

The savior whom God promised would be the victor over Satan, sin, and death, and he would be the victor through his own death and resurrection. No one anticipated the sacrifice of the sinless Savior except the God who planned it all before time began.

To satisfy God's wrath against sin, he requires a blood sacrifice for sins. The Lord prescribed the manner of these sacrifices in detail in his law. "For the life of the flesh is in the blood, and I have given it for you on the altar to make atonement for your souls, for it is the blood that makes atonement by the life" (Lev. 17:11).

But the blood of livestock and poultry could never take away our sins once and for all (Heb. 10:11). That's why the sacrifices had to be offered over and over again. It's like how you have to wash your hands multiple times a day to keep them clean. Between handling raw meat in the kitchen, flushing a toilet, changing a diaper, or picking up snot-covered teething toys, the potential for our hands to become dirty is really overwhelming. There's no way we can keep our hands perfectly clean, even if we use antibacterial hand soap every few minutes. It's still only 99.9 percent effective at killing germs! At least that's what the label says.

Jesus died on the cross to give us clean hearts. Psalm 103:12 says, "As far as the east is from the west, so far does he remove our transgressions from us." When Jesus offered his body on the cross, it was a one-time act. As he died, Jesus said, "It is finished" (John 19:30). Atonement had been made. The sons of men could be forgiven by trusting in the Son of Man who died on their behalf and rose again from the dead.

Jesus redeemed us by fulfilling God's perfect law for us. The law is summarized in the act of perfectly loving God and our neighbors—a law which no one could obey perfectly except Jesus. "And behold, a lawyer stood up to put him to the test, saying, 'Teacher, what shall I do to inherit eternal life?' He said to him, 'What is written in the Law? How do you read it?' And he answered, 'You shall love the Lord your God with all your heart and with all your soul and with all your strength and with all your mind, and your neighbor as yourself.' And he said to him, 'You have answered correctly; do this, and you will live'" (Luke 10:25-28).

We fail to love our husband as we ought, we fail to love our children as we ought, we fail to love our neighbors and friends as we ought, and, most importantly, we fail to love God as we ought.

Only Jesus loved God the Father perfectly and loved his neighbor as he loved himself. When Jesus died on the cross in our place, he became the curse for us. Even though he had no sin, "he himself bore our sins in his body on the tree, that we might die to sin and live to righteousness. By his wounds you have been healed" (1 Pet. 2:24). "For our sake he made him to be sin who knew no sin, so that in him we might become the righteousness of God" (2 Cor. 5:21).

The good news is what *God* has done on behalf of sinners who could never and would never save themselves. The gospel is nothing less than this good news—we preach Christ crucified.

When we believe this good news by faith, repenting of our sin and embracing the free gift of righteousness in Christ, God saves us. God sends his Holy Spirit to dwell inside our hearts and seal us as his for all eternity (2 Cor. 1:22). Christ died according to God's plan in order to bring us to God. That's the good news. "For Christ also suffered once for sins, the righteous for the unrighteous, that he might bring us to God, being put to death in the flesh but made alive in the spirit" (1 Pet. 3:18).

Of course, the good news of what God has done in Jesus *includes* everything Christ has accomplished for us in his work on the cross. But the benefits of Christ's cross work are not the gospel—they are benefits, gifts that lead us to God. Entire books have been written on differentiating the actual good news and the benefits of the good news.[2]

Glimpses of Grace is about how we can treasure the gospel in light of the reality that this good news is true.

Counterfeiting the Gospel

My oldest child is a fact checker by nature. Whenever I send my instructions with a younger child to repeat in the hearing of all the kids, usually the next voice I hear is my fact checker's. "Mo-o-o-m? Did you *really* say . . . ?"

We need to do fact checking when we hear things about the gospel. Part of the apostle Paul's ministry was to "destroy arguments and every lofty opinion raised against the knowledge of God, and take every thought captive to obey Christ" (2 Cor. 10:5). This kind of opinion slaying and bad-idea jailing is still necessary today. The only opinion worth canonizing is the opinion of God himself as it is written in his authoritative Word—the Bible. The only ideas worth promulgating are those found in God's holy Word.

When a stray opinion or idea masquerades as God's gospel or as a benefit of God's gospel, our ears ought to perk up and our minds ought to crank into gear. It is the responsibility of every theologian to check and recheck according to the Scriptures the ideas floating about regarding who God is and what he does and what he desires.

And everyone who thinks about God, in a very practical sense of the word, is a theologian.

Paul told Timothy to guard the gospel: "O Timothy, guard the deposit entrusted to you. Avoid the irreverent babble and contradictions of what is falsely called 'knowledge,' for by professing it some have swerved from the faith" (1 Tim. 6:20–21; see also 2 Tim. 1:14). The stakes of false doctrine are not merely high—they are matters of eternal life and death.

Consider the phrase "gospel identity amnesia."[3] Simply stated, gospel identity amnesia is where you forget the gospel of Jesus and live in the reality of some counterfeit gospel.[4]

How do you know if the gospel you live by is Jesus's gospel? Consider how law enforcers learn to identify illegally printed money. They spend the vast majority of their training learning to recognize counterfeit money by studying the real thing. We can learn to identify false gospels by studying the real thing. We need to examine the gospel from the Scriptures.

Self-Justification Is Not Good News

One of the more popular of the false gospels is self-justification. Major world religions have been built on the idea that humanity can rise above the weaknesses and ailments that beset it. We can absolve ourselves from the evils we commit if we work hard enough and do enough good to outweigh the bad. The false gospel of self-justification is a great enemy of the Christian faith because so many have been misled to believe that it *is* Christianity.

Many of my friends who hold to other religions sincerely believe that our faith is essentially the same. "You do good things, we do good things, and God is merciful. See, we're the same!" But these theologies are not the same. Justifying yourself through good works and being declared righteous because of Christ's good works are in no way similar. We cannot save ourselves and completely depend on a savior at the same time—even when we throw in the weak disclaimer "and God is merciful" to attempt to honor God.

We like to think there is a bottom line of God's righteous standards. We want to be able to "check the box" so our guilty consciences will leave us alone. But there is no bottom line of God's righteousness—he is *infinitely* holy.

When we reject the Son of God, who was sent according to the plan of the Father, and try to save ourselves through good works, we fail to honor God. The Bible says our good deeds are like filthy rags compared to his righteousness. The only thing a filthy rag does for us is rub in the stains of sin and guilt on our consciences.

The Good-Life Formula Is Not Good News

In her book *Practical Theology for Women*, Wendy Alsup says, "Don't be content with the Christian desk calendar approach to Christianity. Don't be satisfied with a daily practical saying or some three-step process for being a good wife or better friend."[5] Not only is this method for living inferior to the gospel, but in the end it can't deliver what God promises in the gospel.

Christianity is not a how-to manual for having a nice life. Paul said in 1 Corinthians 15:19, "If in Christ we have hope in this life only, we are of all people most to be pitied." A life without hope in God's future grace is a pitiful life. Paul says it is the *epitome* of a pitiful life. Jesus's work on the cross means more for you than an example for good living. The Bible is God's story of how he redeems a people he has chosen to worship him for all eternity. Just as an example, the impact of the gospel radically reorients the way you speak to people, *and* its impact on your life reaches much further than the communication problems you have with your spouse.

In the end, the good-life formula will not bring you to God and save you from your sins. Only Jesus does this through the gospel. In its worst work, the good-life formula can help create a delusion that because you are living in a Christian-like manner, you must be pleasing to God. In reality, your righteousness may be like that of the Pharisees, whom Jesus described as whitewashed tombs with dead men's bones inside. In this way, the good-life formula is an offspring of self-justification.

Making Your Own Rules Is Not Good News

If this describes your approach to life, then you have probably lived long enough to discover that you're the only person in your life who fully appreciates your wisdom. The Bible says that "the fear of the LORD is the beginning of knowledge; fools despise wisdom and instruction" (Prov. 1:7). Proverbs 21:2 says, "Every way of a man is right in his own eyes, but the LORD weighs the heart."

The Lord God is just in judging sin, as he is perfectly holy and good. Romans 1 describes people who reject God and the witness of his character:

> For the wrath of God is revealed from heaven against all ungodliness and unrighteousness of men, who by their unrighteousness suppress the truth. For what can be known about God is plain to them, because God has shown it to them. For his invisible attributes, namely, his eternal power and divine nature, have been clearly perceived, ever since the creation of the world, in the things that have been made. So they are without excuse. For although they knew God, they did not honor him as God or give thanks to him, but they became futile in their thinking, and their foolish hearts were darkened. Claiming to be wise, they became fools, and exchanged the glory of the immortal God for images resembling mortal man and birds and animals and creeping things. (Rom. 1:18–23)

It takes deliberate effort to reject God.

Friend, if you have rejected God's rule over your life as I had and these passages in Proverbs and Romans describe you, please listen to Jesus invite you to turn from your sin and hide yourself in him. Jesus said, "I am the way, and the truth, and the life. No one comes to the Father except through me" (John 14:6). The cross is the measure of God's holiness. He is infinitely holy so that only one who is also infinitely holy could atone for sins against the triune God. The cross is the measure of God's willingness to save sinners. The Father is the merciful architect of this plan for salvation, the Son gladly did his Father's will, and the Holy Spirit is delighted to bring everything to fruition. Would you repent of your sin, trusting in Christ even today?

Preaching the Gospel to Yourself

At one point, as I began to walk with Jesus I began to think, "I'm so ready to grow in my faith. What I need is more information about the Bible, and that will do the trick." I gave myself to rigorous study just for the sake of becoming smarter, thinking that reading books by holy people would rub their holiness off on me.

It is quite easy to allow the gospel to become overshadowed by our own efforts to grow spiritually. Spiritual disciplines serve as gateways to cherishing the gospel, not as substitutes for the gospel. D. A. Carson warns us against attempting to live Christianly but relegating the cross to mere insurance against the fires of hell: "First, if the gospel becomes that by which we slip into the kingdom, but all the business of transformation turns on postgospel disciplines and strategies, then we shall constantly be directing the attention of people *away* from the gospel, *away* from the cross and resurrection. Soon the gospel will be something that we quietly assume is necessary for salvation, but not what we are excited about, not what we are preaching, not the power of God."[6] Assuming the gospel but relying on what Carson calls "postgospel disciplines" for life change is like giving the evil Serpent back its teeth. If resisting sin and temptation is up to your own power and discipline, your potential to overcome sin is only as powerful as your own righteousness.

But who of us would rather rely on our own righteousness? Would anyone who is in Christ rather preach something *other* than the gospel? If God's matchless power is available to us, why would we prefer to rely on our inferior strength for personal growth in holiness? Yet this is what we do when we quietly assume the gospel and pull ourselves up by the bootstraps of postgospel disciplines.

So how do we know if we've assumed the gospel? Mack Stiles says so aptly that the way to know if we've assumed the gospel is this: you don't hear it anymore.[7] Everyone talks to themselves. You are even talking to yourself when you think you're not listening. Think about it: What do you say in your mind when you stub your toe? Or hear the phone ring? Or slam on the car brakes to avoid hitting the car in front of you? You talk to yourself.

Now consider weightier issues. What do we tell ourselves when we become aware of our distraction from following God? With what advice do we console ourselves when we feel distant from God? What do we tell ourselves is the solution to our anxiety and restless hearts? Where is the first place we turn when we want to see our lives change? To cut to the chase, are we "attempting to connect with God apart from self-conscious dependence on the substitutionary death and resurrection of Jesus?"[8]

Taking a few minutes to journal your thoughts or trying some audio journaling (using verbal "notes to self" with a voice recorder) are good ways to discover your stream of consciousness if you aren't convinced that you talk to yourself.

We all spend time talking to ourselves, and it matters what we're saying. Are you telling yourself you need to "get religious" and do a better job to please God? Or do you remind yourself that you answer to no one but you?

Paul the Broken Record

My favorite food is chips and salsa. I think I could eat chips and salsa every day and never get bored with it. Granted, I might get sick (literally) from eating so many chips and salsa. But it's my favorite!

The gospel is like that. It should be our favorite thing to hear over and again! And it won't make you sick to your stomach.

A quick scan through Paul's epistles shows us that Paul's favorite method of ministry was through the preaching and repreaching of the gospel—not only to nonbelievers but to believers as well. Over and over again in the epistles he rehearsed the gospel.

> Re-preaching the gospel and then showing how it applied to life was Paul's choice method for ministering to believers, thereby

providing a divinely inspired pattern for me to follow when ministering to myself and to other believers.[9]

In a sermon he preached, Martin Luther made a great case for reminding ourselves often of the gospel and its effects on our lives: "Are you among those who say, 'I have heard [the gospel] all before; why must I hear it again?' If so, your heart has become dull, satiated, and shameless, and this food does not taste good to you. This is the same thing that happened to the Jews in the wilderness when they grew tired of eating manna. But if you are a Christian, you will never grow weary, but will long to hear this message often and to speak about it forever."[10]

The Israelites got tired of eating manna. Have you gotten tired of feasting your soul on the truths of the gospel?

Understanding the Gospel as It Applies to Your Life

All this talk about the gospel begs the question, what's the point? Why should we care about the gospel and how it relates to our everyday lives in the home?

Perhaps you're a committed Christian and you're on board with believing the gospel. You look forward to your daily growth in godliness through the gospel. I hope that this book serves your soul as you gladly submit to God's purposes in making you more like his Son.

But maybe you're one who struggles with doubts. My friend, if you have just a mustard seed of faith that the gospel might contain some help for you in your home, please keep reading.

I realize that you might be thinking that all of this sounds a little smurfy. Perhaps you're skeptical about Jesus's gospel. I want to address these reservations, so I urge you to please keep reading.

I'm excited to explore these ideas with you regardless of where you're coming from. I can't think of anything better to talk about than how we can revel in the extraordinary God who reaches into the lives of sinners who need his grace as they live their ordinary lives in their homes.

3

The Power of Parables

Bridesmaids, sweeping, baking, seeds, birds, gardening, landlords, and neighbors—Jesus talked about all kinds of domestic things.

He used these things to make a point—many points, actually, about his Father and what his kingdom is like. These stories that Jesus used to point us to our heavenly Father are called parables.

Jesus Spoke in Parables

Scripture tells us that Jesus used parables for two purposes. First, he spoke in parables to reveal things. As he spoke in parables, his words sifted through pretense and exposed the heart. He shed light on the everyday moments of our lives and made us see ourselves in the story. In Jesus's parables he paints scenarios where we can look through the lens of our common circumstances to see comparisons between ourselves and God's character, his kingdom, and his activity in the world.

The second thing Jesus did with his parables was to emphasize the point that his teachings were concealed from people who did not understand the things of God. "This is why I speak to them in parables, because seeing they do not see, and hearing they do not hear, nor do they understand" (Matt. 13:13).

Jesus's parables demonstrate that spiritual things are concealed and hidden from people who are blind and deaf to spiritual things. Have you ever been in a classroom setting, in a meeting at work, at dinner with a friend, or in conversation with your spouse, and all of a sudden his or her voice interrupts your train of thought with, "Do you know what I mean?" And it becomes apparent to you and to that other person that you, indeed, do *not* know what they mean. Maybe you tuned out a long time ago. Perhaps in that moment you might blush or ask for clarification. You might even confess to the other person, "I wasn't listening; would you please repeat what you were saying?"

But spiritual blindness and deafness differ from daydreaming or from spiritual Attention Deficit Disorder. This is more than a temporary condition in which the remedy is merely that you need to "just pay attention." You cannot just listen closer or clean your glasses to try to focus better to understand the point of Jesus's parables. When you are spiritually blind or deaf, you have a spiritual disability that prevents you from getting it.

By God's grace, people who do not see or hear the glory of Jesus's teachings have an opportunity to realize that they are blind and deaf spiritually. As we look to God in repentance and faith, the Spirit of God will make us aware that we are blind and deaf to spiritual things. As the Holy Spirit tunes our hearts to grace, we have an opportunity to see how we've been deceived by our sin.

As he propounds "riddles" in his parables, we are made aware of our spiritual poverty. Then when by his grace we are made aware of our spiritual poverty, we can cry out to the Lord in repentance and belief, "Open the eyes of our hearts so that we can know the hope to which you've called us!" As we battle unbelief, may we cry out with the anxiety-filled father who doubted Jesus's ability and willingness to heal his dying daughter, "I believe; help my unbelief!" (Mark 9:24).

"Quiet" Time: An Illustration

Movie theaters often play a little commercial in the premovie show about movie manners and courtesy. A voice tells you to turn your mobile phone ringers to their silent setting and not to talk with your neighbor during the show. And then the colloquial phrase "silence is golden" fills the movie screen in ten-foot-tall letters.

Many of my neighbors here in the Middle East think that idea is just plain silly. How are you to enjoy the movie if you can't make comments and chat with your friend while you're watching it? And if someone calls or texts you, then how rude would you be to "silence" them for the sake of an insignificant, inanimate movie! The idea of watching a movie in solitary silence is lost on cultures that value relationships so highly.

The idea of devotional time as "quiet time" is sort of like this experience at the movie theater. I believe it is helpful and necessary to retreat to quiet places to pray and read God's Word. But silence is not necessary for you to have a vibrant relationship with God.

Your spiritual life is not restricted to early mornings before the noisemakers in your life wake up. If you feel that God meets with you only when the house is empty or quiet, you'll view every noise and every noisemaker as an annoying distraction to your communion with God. Or worse—there are times when I'm tempted to think of my whining toddler or ringing doorbell as obstacles that Satan has put in my way to take my eyes off Jesus.

The temptation is to believe that if you could only transcend this spiritually devoid existence, then you could meet with God on a higher level. This idea is not only practically impossible and pastorally unhelpful, but it is unbiblical as well.

Even so, we must be careful not to swing too far the other way. When we immortalize the material and elevate it to the highest good, we set up idols to worship and pay homage to. This can happen when we attach our reason for being to our current role in life—even roles like being a mother or housewife.

We have so many good things in our lives—home, families, husband and children, friends, work, achievements, and gifts. But if we think these things are god, or if we absolutely have to have these things in order to connect with God, then our heart has manufactured an idol. When any of these good things turns into something we resent or complain about because we feel it is an obstacle to fellowship with God, our heart has manufactured an idol.

As Thomas Oden said so poignantly, "Every self exists in relation to values perceived as making life worth living." Even as we make it our aim to do all things with excellence and be good stewards of our home and children, our focus can easily be shifted to "whatever you do, do all to promote your own glory."

This is a good opportunity to test ourselves. We should frequently ask ourselves (and ask our friends to ask us as well), is your role or identity as a homemaker the object of your affections? Do you lose your cool when that identity is threatened? Do you serve your image of a good mother? Are you controlled by the things you feel you need in order to achieve or maintain your role?

Both of these un-Christian worldviews—God is detested with the mundane and the mundane is my god—are deceptive and destructive. When our hearts are saturated in these lies, we cease to live in a way that honors God. Some of us are spiritually sleepy, and we need to wake up to the reality of the implications of the gospel. Some of us need to believe the gospel for the first time. Either way, we all need to submit to the expulsive power of a greater affection that is found only in Christ.

Solitude or Circus—Jesus Is with You

One of my kids' favorite books is a brilliant little board book by Debby Anderson called *Jesus Is with Me*. The book is meant to be read (or sung) aloud to the tune of "Jingle Bells." Anderson draws adorable children from different ethnicities in different scenarios—on a bus, in a car—and talks about how Jesus is with them no matter where they are. One of the lines goes like this: "On a boat, that will float, Jesus is with me."

My kids have read this book so many times that they have ad-libbed lines based on the tune and the concept. Neither me nor my husband can carry a tune in a bucket, but somehow our girls learned to sing. One of my girls sang in the bath one night, "In the tub, rub-a-dub, Jesus is with me." Then she thoughtfully added,

"Oh, and he's with you, too, Mommy. Even though you're sitting on the potty." (I should clarify that the toilet seat was down!)

I just think it's wonderful to teach children that fellowship with Christ is not constrained to formally religious experiences or places. My kids believe that is true. Jesus is with us everywhere we go because he rules over the world he's created, and he indwells those who believe in him.

But something happens to us big people who get mired down with the tyranny of the urgent in the things we can see. How easy is it for us to relegate Jesus's influence over us to one spot in our house under specific circumstances and only for a certain period of time each day!

Peace and quiet are not ultimate. Activity and responsibility are not ultimate. Because Christ is ultimate, the loss of any of these things—solitude or circus—makes no difference in the sufficiency of Christ or in his ability to give you everything you need for life and godliness. First Peter 1:15–16 says, "But as he who called you is holy, you also be holy in all your conduct, since it is written, 'You shall be holy, for I am holy.'"

God is holy, and he fellowships with us as we are in the midst of our mundane. The Son of God entered his own creation, after all. The Eternal One who was before all things and in whom all things hold together became a human being.

When we're tempted to either despise our everyday lives or worship our everyday lives, we need to remember what Paul said in Romans 12:1–2: "I appeal to you therefore, brothers, by the mercies of God, to present your bodies as a living sacrifice, holy and acceptable to God, which is your spiritual worship. Do not be conformed to this world, but be transformed by the renewal of your mind, that by testing you may discern what is the will of God, what is good and acceptable and perfect." Life in the body, when presented to the Lord as a living sacrifice because of his mercy, is holy and acceptable in his sight.

Living your everyday life for God's sake is spiritual worship.

But we need to have mental overrides in order to do this. Our natural inclination is to believe the lies of the world and conform ourselves, our homes, our families, and our desires to what we see in the world. Only by renewing our minds through the Word of God, which works in us, can we discern how we might honor God in our homes.

Pass everything the world presents you through the sieve of the Word of God—what does God's Word say about it? And take pains to have the Word of God work in you as well. As you read God's Word he will delight in showing you what is good and acceptable and perfect. Ask God to renew your mind according to his Word, and he will do it! I can't say whether this mind renewal will solve the problem of forgetful "mommy brain," though. As you walk into the kitchen for the umpteenth time in a day and forget why you were there in the first place, you'll at least be able to discern that God's will for you might not be to curse your mommy brain and vow to write down your to-do list in permanent marker on your forearms.

How the Word of God Works in Us

Oh, how I would love to dwell on the great magnitude of the glory of God all day long. I would love for my soul to believe on the precious promises of God at all times. But the reality is that we live in a fallen world, and we are, indeed, still sinners.

The centrality of "me" in our lives takes precedence over meditating on the grandeur of the Holy One. We're also easily distracted with things of eternal insignificance and obsess over petty trivialities. To take an example from my own life this afternoon, I found myself with some extra time, so I purposed to pray. I sat down on a couch in my home and immediately my mind was transfixed on whether that couch ought to have two pillows or three plus a throw blanket. Here I was with free, unlimited access to the throne room of the Most High because of Jesus's blood-bought gift of reconciliation with God. And all I could think about was *pillows*. To illustrate how important the pillow problem was to me, I'll confess that my mind came back to this great pillow dilemma every time I passed by that particular couch tonight. (I eventually ended up switching a pillow out from another room and added a throw blanket to the couch, in case this dilemma left you hanging!)

This illustration of me struggling to pray one afternoon is just a tiny microcosm of the overarching struggle of our Christian lives. We want to consciously live in the reality of the gospel and behold our God (Isa. 40:9). In our living and in our beholding, there is great joy to be found! But the cares of this world can be petty and urgent—or serious and urgent!

Walking with God in a world like this one can feel so complicated sometimes. I know that my problem that night was really not the pillows but a complex host of reasons that led me to believing the pillows were more important than fellowship with God. Hebrews 12:1–2 says we need to lay aside every weight and sin so that we can run with endurance the race set before us, looking to Jesus. This "weight" includes good things that become unhelpful things—like obsessions over petty trivialities. And, of course, "sin" includes things that hinder our running because they are sinful.

Seeing the brilliance of the cross and embracing its message are at the core of how God wants to work in our mundane to bring glory to himself.

As we consider the truth of God's Word and receive it by faith, the Word *works in us* (1 Thess. 2:13). The Bible describes so many metaphors of the way God's indwelling Holy Spirit uses God's Word to work in us. One domestic example is fruit. Most of us just go to a grocery store to buy fruit that is generally available in ample supply and neatly arranged in bins ready to be taken home and eaten. Most of us forget that fruit is the result of an arduous process—tilling soil, planting seeds, watering plants, fending off bugs, and waiting for harvest.

When we apprehend the pride-imploding beauty of what Jesus did on the cross, we don't want to have anything to do with all the things that bloat our egos. When we are engaged in seeing and savoring the beauty of Jesus, the vain things that charm us most fade away into the distance.

When we see the holiness of the God whom the Bible calls "a consuming fire," we realize the rags of our self-righteous deeds are not adequate coverings for us. When we have faith in Christ, who absorbed the Father's wrath for our sin on the cross, we no longer bear that sin. Instead, we find ourselves clothed in the righteousness of Christ and seated at Jesus's feet "in our right minds." The transforming nature of this gospel has a radical impact on our mundane lives. Many of us go through our Christian lives discouraged by an underrealized perspective of our sanctification. Life change is often disregarded as impossible to do so why try, or is thought of as entirely possible if we only put our minds to it (and have the right tools and books available). This has a radical impact on how we speak to our children when we're tired and would rather roll over in bed and catch some more shut-eye. This has a radical impact on how we jockey for the shortest line at the grocery store. Living in the reality of the gospel means the difference between complaining to others about something that annoys us and rejoicing in the Lord's faithfulness to his name.

We need to remind ourselves to live in the reality of this gospel each day. But the practice of preaching the gospel to yourself doesn't mean that you just give yourself mini-sermons when you feel your faith wavering. No, it means that you see things as an opportunity to talk with God, talk about God, and receive wisdom from the Bible throughout your day.

This means that your faith looks forward to the promises of God fulfilled for you forever; at the same time your faith looks backward to the cross and believes that Christ's death has purchased those promises for you.

Why Does God Want to Use the Mundane?

When I say the words, "the gift of God," what do you think about? Perhaps your children's smiling, grape jelly–smeared faces come to mind. Or your mind's eye may glance over to the framed picture of you and your husband on your wedding day. Or you might be sitting in a nice chair, relaxing in the home you've worked hard to be able to enjoy. All these things would certainly be gifts of God. They are gifts "of" God in the sense that they are *from* him to be enjoyed *by* you *for* his glory.

But in a very real sense, when we say "the gift of God," we are actually saying the gift is God himself. God is *good*. "And he said, 'I will make all my goodness pass before you and will proclaim before you my name "The Lord." And I will be gracious to whom I will be gracious, and will show mercy on whom I will show mercy'" (Ex. 33:19). He is the ultimate good.

Does God just want us to be happy about our life's circumstances? Does God just want us to have good attitudes while we are rinsing soiled bedsheets for the third time in one week? Does God just want us to think of our life as "glass half full"? *Is that all God wants?* Many people think that this is the goal of the Christian life. And by the way some people write and speak, you could easily think that circumstantial optimism is the very essence of the Christian faith.

Surely these things—a cheerful attitude and sense of hopefulness—are wonderful by-products of rejoicing in God while in the midst of our homes. But that's just what they are—by-products.

The source of our faith, hope, love, joy, and gospel-grounded optimism is *God himself* and not our stuff or our circumstances. Isaiah 61:10 says, "I will greatly rejoice in the Lord; my soul shall exult in my God, for he has clothed me with the garments of salvation; he has covered me with the robe of righteousness, as a bridegroom decks himself like a priest with a beautiful headdress, and as a bride adorns herself with her jewels."

God wants to use our lives in the home to glorify himself and lead us to worship him because he is the ultimate treasure who is worthy of all of our affections, attention, preoccupation, and strength.

Let me put it another way. God is good, he does good things, and he gives us good gifts to enjoy. *But why?* To whom is the praise, affection, preoccupation, worship, and joy directed in Psalm 103:1–5?

> Bless the LORD , O my soul,
> and all that is within me,
> bless his holy name!
> Bless the LORD, O my soul,
> and forget not all his benefits,
> who forgives all your iniquity,
> who heals all your diseases,
> who redeems your life from the pit,
> who crowns you with steadfast love and mercy,
> who satisfies you with good
> so that your youth is renewed like the eagle's. (Ps. 103:1–5)

This worship is directed to God—"Bless the LORD."

Why Is Fruit So Sweet?

Of course, as Christians we enjoy the fruits of abiding in Jesus. We relish relationships in which forgiveness is valued and grace is extended. But the point in forgiving one another is not just about the act of forgiving—it is the aim or goal that forgiveness seeks, which is reconciliation with God. It's the same way with God and his great gospel. The forgiveness of our sins is a gift of his grace, but it's not "the" gift. "The" gift God offers us through Jesus's work on the cross is everlasting fellowship with a holy God.

"Christ also suffered once for sins, the righteous for the unrighteous, that he might bring us to God" (1 Pet. 3:18). Jesus's substitutionary death on the cross forgives our sin—so that he might bring us to God. "For our sake he made him to be sin who knew no sin, so that in him we might become the righteousness of God"

(2 Cor. 5:21). Jesus's righteous perfections imputed to us declare us holy as he is holy—so that he might bring us to God.

Jesus did all this so we might be free to enjoy God forever. In the moments before he was betrayed Jesus prayed for his disciples in John 17. In verse 3 Jesus defines eternal life: "And this is eternal life, that they know you the only true God, and Jesus Christ whom you have sent." And in verses 20–26 Jesus prays that his disciples would have unity with one another and with God. Jesus reiterated his request in verse 24, which is the most loving request Jesus could have made on our behalf: "Father, I desire that they also, whom you have given me, may be with me where I am, to see my glory that you have given me because you loved me before the foundation of the world."

Enjoy God in Your Home

Jesus apparently believes that the most satisfying thing for us in all eternity is to behold his glory in his very presence.

He is not absent from our noisy, chaotic lives. He is with us, even to the end of the age (Matt. 28:20). And if he's with us even to the end of the age, then he is with us even to the end of our carpooling route. He's with us even to the end of the meat in the fridge when grocery day isn't for another four days. He's with us even to the end of a long night of waking with a crying baby. He's with us even to the end of a party that we'd rather not be at or be hosting, for whatever reason. He's with us even to the end of a hectic morning of rushing around trying to get out the door. He's with us even to the end of a dreadful day when nothing seemed to go as planned.

Now let's go see how the presence of God makes the difference in the way we live our lives in the home and how the gospel of Jesus Christ has given us this supreme gift.

4

Christ in You,
the Hope of Glory

It's tempting to view everyday life merely as a monotonous cycle of making the beds only to lie in them again. Even the preacher in the book of Ecclesiastes lamented the monotony of the mundane: "Vanity of vanities, says the Preacher, vanity of vanities! All is vanity. What does man gain by all the toil at which he toils under the sun? . . . All things are full of weariness; a man cannot utter it; the eye is not satisfied with seeing, nor the ear filled with hearing. What has been is what will be, and what has been done is what will be done, and there is nothing new under the sun" (Eccles. 1:2–3, 8–9).

When God's activity in the world means very little to us, we're functionally hopeless. When everything is vanity, nothing makes sense or brings us joy. The fact that "Jesus Christ is the same yesterday and today and forever" (Heb. 13:8) seems irrelevant.

"Nothing ever changes," we grumble. The dishes will always reappear in the sink and Mount Laundry will always be erupting in cotton blends. All is vanity.

Recently we hosted our friends from the States for a week-long vacation here in Dubai. My husband, who is the consummate tour guide, loves to show off our city. On one occasion our families went to an aquarium and ate lunch at a café that is themed to look like a jungle. The restaurant is decorated with trees, the ceiling is covered in vines, and there are animatronic jungle animals hiding in every corner.

Every ten minutes or so during our meal we were entertained

by a show of lights and sounds as the animals "came alive"—tigers growling, elephants trumpeting, and gorillas yelling. Statues lit up and moved, and sometimes the show mimicked a thunderstorm! The children were amazed, and we big kids enjoyed watching the children's reactions.

But the most interesting thing about our lunch wasn't the jungle show. It was the family seated at the table next to ours—a mom, a dad, and a preschool-age child. They were not enjoying the ambiance of the café. The child was watching cartoons on a portable DVD player while his mom spooned macaroni into his mouth. Dad was engrossed in a newspaper. The lightning show came on, but instead of trembling with excitement like all the other kids in the café, the little boy told his mom to give him a new cartoon. A few minutes later the animated monkey that hung a few feet above their table began to swing on a vine and do monkey yells. Instead of shrieking with delight, the boy demanded a different cartoon than the one he had just chosen.

Later, in a moment of philosophical reflection, my husband and I talked about how we're not too different from that little boy. Sometimes even the most amusing things bring no relief to the monotony of the mundane. *Wallowing* is the word that comes to mind. Everything is vanity when you're wallowing in boredom. Maybe this scene from the jungle-themed café reminds you of your spiritual life, too. Your soul is so tired of running a spiritual rat race that nothing brings you joy anymore. Especially not the things you do in your home each and every day. You might be apathetic toward your work in the home. Or you might even resent it.

No Testimony of Grace Is Truly Boring

Sometimes when I hear people share their testimony of how they came to believe in Christ, they'll give this disclaimer: "Oh, my testimony isn't anything interesting." Then they'll talk about how they've believed in God for as long as they can remember. Or they were part of a church during their childhood and grew up trusting

Jesus. Or they testify to God's merciful providence in their never having fallen into any scandalous, family-splitting, relationship-severing, lawbreaking sin. Then they'll repeat their disclaimer as a conclusion: "So my story is pretty average and boring." But the Bible begs to differ:

> He has delivered us from the domain of darkness and transferred us to the kingdom of his beloved Son, in whom we have redemption, the forgiveness of sins. (Col. 1:13–14)

> And you, who were dead in your trespasses and the uncircumcision of your flesh, God made alive together with him, having forgiven us all our trespasses, by canceling the record of debt that stood against us with its legal demands. This he set aside, nailing it to the cross. (Col. 2:13–14)

Being delivered from Satan, sin, and death is anything but average or boring. Having your sins forgiven and being redeemed and made alive is mind-boggling. The idea that anyone's testimony of blood-bought salvation could be uninteresting or unspectacular is a defamation of the work of Christ.

Your testimony may have occurred in the most ordinary of circumstances, but behind the scenes a spiritual battle was taking place. The Holy Spirit of God peeled the scales from your spiritually blind eyes, awakened your soul to the bright light of the gospel in the face of Jesus Christ, and breathed life into your lifeless soul. God rescued you from the domain of darkness—however gilded or ordinary or innocent it seemed. Then God transferred you into the kingdom of his beloved Son.

No testimony that involves the Son of God bearing your sins on the cross in order to bring you to God could ever be mundane or boring. It's an epic birth story—a born-again birth story.

The morning my second daughter, Norah, was born began just like every other morning. I rolled my large self over and turned off the alarm clock. Then the birth pangs began before I sat up. I managed the contractions by myself for a little while, then I woke up my husband, my oldest daughter, and my friend Amber who was staying with us. I said, "Time to go!" An hour or so after we got to the hospital, Norah was born. Even though the details aren't dramatic in and of themselves, *Norah* is the crowning glory of that story. The fact that she was born is what makes that story special and anything but ordinary.

The miracle of being born again in Christ Jesus is a birth story that is anything but ordinary. Never get over the grace of God in choosing to give you eternal life! Marvel at the magnitude of God's mercy to save sinners. Cherish the Son of God's willingness to die on your behalf so that you might be born again by faith. Rejoice that the Holy Spirit of God now dwells in you. How can your testimony be blasé?

God's sovereign, undeserved grace makes your story special and anything but ordinary.

Don't Lose What's Been Entrusted to You

I know firsthand that even though my life is hidden in Christ with God, I am so prone to discouragement. My sensitivity to the Holy Spirit is quenched by my sin. My joy in the Lord can be diverted by pain. My wonder in God's character can be dulled by apathy.

When left unchecked, these feelings and tendencies dilute my hope, deceive my heart, and discourage my faith. I have to combat the lies that are presented to me every day by reminding myself of the hope of glory I have in Christ.

Just this afternoon I was thinking about a conflict that my husband and I are helping to resolve between two parties. The more I thought about it, the more skeptical I became. But just an hour earlier I had been rejoicing over how the circumstances seemed ideal for the conflict to be resolved very soon! What changed? I lost sight of the gospel.

We easily lose sight of the gospel. That's why Paul's advice to Timothy is critical for our spiritual health: "Follow the pattern of the sound words that you have heard from me, in the faith and love that are in Christ Jesus. By the Holy Spirit who dwells within us, guard the good deposit entrusted to you" (2 Tim. 1:13–14). The indwelling Holy Spirit enables us to guard the "good deposit," which is the gospel. We can guard the gospel by remembering it, studying it, speaking of it, and applying it.

We Need to See God

The reason for guarding the gospel and applying the gospel is the same—the gospel is the means by which we can behold the glory of God. The law, though perfect and good, cannot give us unhindered vision into the throne room of the Most High, because we can't obey it perfectly. The problem is not with the law; the problem is with us.

After God told Moses, "I will make all my goodness pass before you and will proclaim before you my name 'The Lord.' And I will be gracious to whom I will be gracious, and will show mercy on whom I will show mercy," he said, "You cannot see my face, for man shall not see me and live" (Ex. 33:19–20). When Moses descended Mount Sinai with the Ten Commandments, his face shone with the glory of the Lord, and the Israelites were terrified. So he hid his face with a veil.

Paul explains how we can behold the glory of the Lord because of the gospel. "And we all, with unveiled face, beholding the glory of the Lord, are being transformed into the same image from one degree of glory to another. For this comes from the Lord who is the Spirit" (2 Cor. 3:18). The very sight of Christ in his glory is transforming. When the Holy Spirit of God reveals to us the glory of God in the face of Christ, we are transformed. There is no need to veil our faces, because we are in Christ, and he has given us the spiritual acuity we need in order to behold the Lord's glory.

In this beholding of the Lord, we find the greatest joy imaginable and supreme glory that no eye has seen and no ear has heard. "From of old no one has heard or perceived by the ear, no eye has seen a God besides you, who acts for those who wait for him"

(Isa. 64:4). "Behold your God!" is the most loving command we could receive from the Lord. He is beautiful beyond our human capacity to describe, yet he exuberantly instructs his people to declare his glory:

> Go on up to a high mountain,
>   O Zion, herald of good news;
> lift up your voice and strength,
>   O Jerusalem, herald of good news;
>   lift it up, fear not;
> say to the cities of Judah,
>   "Behold your God!" (Isa. 40:9)

The reason "Behold your God" is good news is that Jesus Christ made it possible for us to see God and live. Without his mediation on our behalf, we may not see God and live. In Christ, we can see God and live *forever*.

Labor to Study Christ

That's why Richard Sibbes recommended that we ought to take pains "to study Christ." We study Christ because we've been saved for the purpose of being transformed into his image, and in our beholding, the work of transformation occurs. "If it is so that we are changed into the image of the second Adam, Jesus Christ, then let us labor every day more and more to study Christ, so that by beholding him we may be transformed into his likeness. The sight of Christ is a transforming sight."[1]

We study Christ because, as we are being transformed into his image, we should like to recognize him when see him in the mirror. And later, when we meet him face-to-face! "For now we see in a mirror dimly, but then face to face. Now I know in part; then I shall know fully, even as I have been fully known" (1 Cor. 13:12).

Our dear friends have adopted all five of their children, and all five of these children are of a different ethnicity than their parents. Their children are not a combination of their physical DNA. But do they resemble their parents? You bet they do! Take one of their sons, for example. Just like his Momma, he has serious issues with any injustice he perceives. At seven years old, he said that if he were the president of his class he would give more time off to the janitor who works too hard. And just like his Daddy, if he's upset with something, then humor goes a long way to help him lighten up.

We inherit character traits and learn behavior from our parents. All the time I find myself saying things that my parents said. I learned how to communicate expectations from Mom and Dad. When my sisters and I were little and Mom took us somewhere, we would get a pep talk in the car. Mom would turn around and announce to us in the backseat, "Now, I want all three of you to behave like the young ladies that I know you are." Sometimes Dad's standards seemed more reasonable, depending on the day: "Let's all try to act like humans."

For some people the remark, "You're just like your mother [or father]," is enough to pick a fight. For a Christian, the greatest testimony of God's grace in our lives is the observation, "You're just like your Father." Being conformed to the image of Christ is God's will for our lives.

We Actively Receive God's Grace

Being conformed to the image of Christ is not an entirely passive activity, like receiving a set of genes upon conception or someone's family name in adoption.

While salvation is initiated by God, we are not passive recipients of his grace. Jonathan Edwards called this grace "efficacious," which speaks of its effectiveness and ability to accomplish God's purposes in our lives. This efficacious grace implies work on our part. As Edwards described it, "In efficacious grace we are not merely passive, nor yet does God do some, and we do the rest. *But God does all, and we do all. God produces all, and we act all.* . . . We are, in different respects, wholly passive, and wholly active."[2] This change is 100 percent initiated by God, 100 percent dependent on the work of Christ, and 100 percent administered by the Holy Spirit.

God's efficacious grace could be described in terms of the different ways you put pajamas on a baby. My son prefers to streak after he takes baths. He even tries to climb out of the tub early before everyone is soaped up and rinsed in order to increase his odds of getting to run around in his birthday suit.

But it's all fun and games until a naked baby has an accident on the carpet, so I quickly chase him down to put on his diaper. Some nights he runs away shrieking and hides under tables and behind chairs trying to avoid the inevitable. Some nights he quietly lies on the bed while I diaper him, and he might even stretch his legs into the pajamas I hold up.

Either way, whether I have to wrestle his clothes onto him or he peacefully submits to the work I am doing, that boy has never gone to bed without a diaper and pajamas on. Of course, we should love to submit to God's efficacious grace as he purposes to make us more like Christ! But sometimes we're like a naked baby hiding behind the couch, reluctant to hold still and thankfully allow God to work in our hearts and get us ready for what he has next.

Our growth in holiness is initiated and produced by God, and we are to actively pursue holiness. The Bible uses some physically laden descriptions of our participation in grace: we "walk in love," "run the race," and "fight the fight of faith." You get the idea that growing in grace is sweaty, hard work. God works in us as we work out our own salvation. "Therefore, my beloved, as you have always obeyed, so now, not only as in my presence but much more in my absence, work out your own salvation with fear and trembling, for it is God who works in you, both to will and to work for his good pleasure" (Phil. 2:12–13).

This kind of grace frees us to love God! Because Christ acquired salvation for us, we can pray as Augustine did, "Give me the grace to do as you command, and command me to do what you will! . . . When your commands are obeyed, it is from you that we receive the power to obey them."[3]

The 20/20 Perspective of Eternity

I think we might all be excited about the potential of grace in our lives to grow us, change us, and make us more like Christ. Perhaps our problem is that the alternatives to growing in grace are sometimes more attractive than the hard work, awkwardness, and even the pain of pursuing holiness. We are sinful; we tend toward apathy in regard to holiness.

We all make choices every day, and it's in these millions of little choices that our character is made. Are you one who chooses hard work, awkwardness, and pain for the sake of growing in Christ? Or are you one who prefers spiritual stagnation and makes corresponding choices? It helps to have a perspective that takes eternity into account when we make decisions. For example, if you wear glasses or contact lenses it's not a good idea to put on makeup without them. Your depth perception is skewed, and you can't see the details or the big picture of your whole face. The worst thing that could happen if you put on your makeup without your glasses on is that you might poke yourself in the cheek with a mascara wand or use eyeliner on your lips. Those kinds of mistakes are humorous and at most embarrassing.

But what if you reach for the nail-polish remover when you were aiming for the eye-makeup remover? You could land yourself in the waiting room at the doctor's office in a world of hurt. That kind of mistake is more painful than embarrassing.

And what if you need corrective lenses to drive and you fail to use them while driving? Now you're breaking the law. The consequences could be deadly if you were in a car accident. The consequences for a mistake like this are far more serious and devastating.

Doing things that require accurate vision can have horrific results if you fail to use the assistance you need. So it is with the decisions we make every day in regard to our growth in holiness. When our perspective of this life is nearsighted, we come to believe that what is in front of us is all there is. We resist doing the awkward things entailed in walking in love. We despise the hard work it takes to run the race. We avoid the pain that results from fighting for our faith by choosing not to fight at all.

We're like that little boy in the café who was surrounded by wonderful things that were designed to delight him. But for lack of a better metaphor, he was already full. There was no more room in his imagination because perhaps it had been dulled, shrunken, and disappointed.

We have opportunities every day to delight in God. We're surrounded by the circumstances he has ordained for our sanctification. God's grace to us in Christ gives us assurance to follow him where he leads, even when it's into awkwardness, hard work, and pain. But every day we ignore the instruments that God would use in our lives to make us holy. If we're not ignoring them, then we may worship them as God instead.

God's triumphant grace in the work of Christ on the cross assures us of this: when our hope is in God's glory, for ourselves and others, then our life in the home is anything but dull, diminutive, and disappointing.

That conclusion sounds lofty, hyperspiritual, and smurfy, but its implications are diffused into our everyday lives much more profusely than you might think. That's what the rest of this book is about.

Part 2

The Miraculous in the Mundane

5

Divine Power and Precious Promises for the 2 a.m. Feeding

I had heard that the transition from having two kids to three would be more difficult than going from zero to one or from one to two. But this was ridiculous.

I Don't Think I Can Take Much More of This

The day we brought Judson home from the hospital it was game on. My daughters, nearly four years old and two years old at the time, were anxious to spend time with me and their wrinkly, wiggly baby brother. The girls' grandparents and our friends had taken excellent care of them for the past few days. But the girls had just about reached their limit of time away from Mommy.

I transferred the dirty laundry from my hospital bag into the hamper, and I relaxed on my bed with my newborn in my arms. Even though the girls had already spent time with Judson at the hospital, they climbed onto our tall bed like hyper little mountain goats just to be near him. "I want to see him, let me see him!" "No! Me turn!" "Mommy, she's kicking me. Make her stop!" "Me-e-e!" They were doing that smothering thing that they do so well. Limbs were clamoring all over the place, and somehow the baby got jostled. He started crying.

"Aw, baby brother is crying; come here, baby." My oldest got her arms underneath his tiny body and started pulling him toward her. "Oh, no, Sweetie, be gentle; Mommy's got him." Norah wasn't about to let Aliza get all of the baby-holding action, so she got in on the tug of war, too.

It all happened so fast. Judson was crying, Aliza wouldn't let go, and Norah in a moment of desperation leaned in and squealed into the baby's face, "Ah-h-h-h-h!" For a second all was silent. Then the baby's eyes widened, and he cried like his heart had been broken. I blurted out, "Everybody. Get. *Off!*" Shocked by my harsh tone, the girls untangled themselves and slipped out of my lap and off the bed. They stood quietly by my side. "Sorry, Mommy," Aliza whispered. Norah, who wasn't much for words at the time, just stared up at me with a penitent look from under her long eyelashes, tears rolling down her cheeks.

"Mommy's sorry, girls. Mommy's sorry, too." I could feel my face getting warm and tears blearing my eyes. "Mommy needs some time alone for a few minutes. Play in your room quietly, please." The girls shuttled themselves out of my bedroom and into theirs. In between my son's shrill, newborn cries I could hear the girls still arguing with each other through the baby monitor. "Mi-i-i-i-i-ne! My doll!" "I'm playing with it right now, so it's mine!" One by one the tears slid down my cheeks. How was I supposed to do this? It's Day One at home and—no, it's *Hour* One—and I can't even cope. What kind of a mother am I who shouts at her kids who just want to get to know their new brother?

Fluctuating levels of hormones were at play after an emotional birth. In my volunteer work as a birth doula, I frequently discuss this initial postpartum phase and encourage ladies not to be surprised that they experience mood swings when they bring their babies home.

I knew things would adjust to a new normal eventually, but my heart didn't want to buy it. The pride that would not allow me to extend grace to myself was symptomatic of a deeper problem.

A Deeper Problem

Fast-forward four months. Judson's little buddies who were born around the same time were all sleeping through the night. One by one their moms announced to the world, "Wow! My baby slept ten hours straight! I feel like a new woman!" But nighttime sleep still eluded us. My son was perfectly healthy, but he wasn't willing to go two or three hours without feeding. I managed to get through the nights on determined gratitude, thankful that I had a sweet baby to take care of.

Then Judson started struggling with gas pains the first night my husband was gone on a trip for work. The baby would feed, cry, spit up, cry, nap for an hour, repeat. I frantically tried every trick in the book—gas drops, tummy rubs, warm towels, anything I could think to do in the middle of the night.

After a short sleep, at 5 a.m. I heard the baby rustling around in his bassinet. In a few moments he would wake up and start to cry. He did, so I fed him, burped him, and he started to doze back to sleep. What luck! No rocking or shushing this time! I laid him down.

Just then Judson let out a high-pitched cry. Gas pain. He was writhing around in his swaddling blanket, his brow scrunched up in frustration. I got out of bed again for what seemed like the thousandth time that night. I stood over his crib, lifted him out, and held his tensed body over my shoulder and tried to gently burp him. He belched, and I could feel warm, wet spit-up drip down my back and heard it splash onto the floor.

"Are you *kidding* me!" I don't know who my outburst was intended for. It just seemed like the right thing to say in the moment. My sweet baby just kept crying. I cried, too. And prayed the only prayer I could, "God, help me."

Then I saw sunlight peeking out from under the curtains. It was almost time to wake up. My alarm clock would go off in minutes, and the girls would clamor out of bed ready to party. Thoughts of another hectic morning and busy day without a break assaulted me and I cried bitter tears. Where is God? How could God do this to me? How does he expect me to face this day?

As the sun got brighter and brighter and I felt another wave of fatigue wash over me, I made a resolution. I resolved to organize my circumstances better to alleviate some of the pressure. Get the kids on a better nap schedule, sort out a cleaning routine, and get my spiritual disciplines in order. Maybe then I would feel closer to God again, when my house is in better order. But something inside me said that controlling my circumstances wouldn't fill the void in my soul. You can't organize your way into communion with God.

I Really Can't Take This Anymore

Does my story sound at all familiar to you? Maybe you feel like your life is suffocating you. Perhaps you don't have sleepless nights or a gassy baby who needs you, but maybe your circumstances dictate how you feel and how you relate to God. You're trapped in an endless cycle, and you can't see any way out. You've prayed about it, and you deeply regret that you don't meet God's standard of holiness in the midst of your circumstances.

You muscle through the days and pray the nights pass quickly. You lack thankfulness to God for the gifts he's given you; you avoid reflecting on the day out of guilt over your failures. You fantasize about how other women live, your prayers lack emotional attachment to your heavenly Father, and you feel lost.

You're right. You *can't* do this anymore, and neither can I.

Longing for a connection with God but feeling trapped in the mundane is the story of my life too. But I'm here to tell you there's hope for you to change, and God wants to meet you there. Right there. With spit-up dripping down your back and salty, bitter tear stains on your cheeks. He loves you, he's with you, and he offers you the gift of himself to enjoy forever.

Whatever the "this" that you desperately feel you can't do anymore, it's ultimately not about your circumstances. It's about peace with God. And God has provided a way for you to have that peace that dominates any and all circumstances, regardless of how difficult they are.

The Desperation of Our Circumstances

But this peace is so elusive, isn't it? That's because there are two different ways we typically try to deal with this problem. I'll speak from my own experiences, and perhaps you can relate to one (or both) of my tactics.

One way to cope with my lack of peace and joy is to just forget about it. Just forgetting about it sounds like this—"How silly of me to think that I could have peace and joy during this season of my life. Other women I know are struggling with the same lack of peace and joy. It is just a season, after all, so I shouldn't let it bother me so much. I needn't get frustrated."

Another way to cope with my lack of peace and joy is to work harder. This is usually my poison of choice. I know I can "do life" better if I just set my mind to it. I create charts to organize myself; I schedule everything from naps to meals to chores. I control the variables. I search for a better solution—reading books and blogs— and I solicit the opinions of women whose lifestyles I admire. I turn to more coffee and healthier eating habits. Then one by one these things begin to enslave me. They become burdens. There's always a better way to organize your home, there's always a more ideal routine for your baby, there will always be something else you want but don't have, and you'll never feel like you can drink enough coffee. If you've never tried it before, you're just going to have to trust me on that last one.

Taking a chill pill, relaxing your standards, and letting the kids skip a bath once in awhile can help on a practical level. Schedules and charts and a healthy diet can also help. But if you are depending on these things to fix your life, then you're just putting Band-Aids on a gunshot wound.

The fact is that none of us truly ignores the ache in our souls. We all try to fill it with something. And if you're a Christian or someone who appreciates the wisdom of the Bible, you might try to alleviate the ache with a biblically based prescription: more time in prayer. More Bible reading. More discipline. All of these things are good.

The Pharisees thought so, too. And what scares me is that *that is so like me.* Just like the Pharisees I think I can manipulate God into my debt if I follow all the rules and engage in stricter spiritual practices.

What makes the difference between that and engaging in spiritual disciplines to grow closer to God is grace. Self-righteousness comes from within us and leads us to worship ourselves. Grace comes from God and leads us to worship him. Both of these scenarios are troubling. Both neglecting what God has called me to do and doing it in my own power are rejections of the grace offered to me through Jesus. If I want to live by grace through faith, then whether I ought to stop these sinful practices is not in question.

The questions I ought to be asking are these: *How* does believing in Jesus change the way I face the monotonous daily grind? Or how does believing take an interrupted nap in stride? *How* does faith in God rescue me from a restless heart? *How* can I experience the peace of Christ when I am so prone to failure because of my sin? *How* does the gospel make me into a woman who rests in the peace of God in the midst of the chaos in my heart?

The Grace in Which We Stand

When you just can't see how you can go on, or you notice that you have become obsessed or overwhelmed by your circumstances, cling to Jesus.

Jesus knew his calling, and he trusted the one who gave it to him. Jesus never sold out when he was tempted to be engaged in something else that wasn't his job. Jesus faithfully endured to the end despite the most difficult circumstances. And Jesus died for you. You can trust him.

His perfect life and sacrificial death are more than just examples for us to follow. He is our righteousness. His death brings us peace with God. And his resurrection guarantees us life.

Believing the gospel gives us courage to repent of these attitudes when we sense them creeping into our souls: (1) The despair of the martyr's mentality; and (2) The pride that grows out of successfully controlling our environments.

Through God's grace, an entirely different dynamic is at work when we look to Jesus for strength and hope. This is faith working through love (Gal. 5:5–6). God in his grace can transform us into those who are steadfast, immovable, always abounding in his work, knowing that in him our labor is not in vain (1 Cor. 15:58).

The One Who Lifted His Arms and Those Who Lift Our Arms

The story in Exodus 17:8–13 is so precious to our family. We remember it often, I think particularly because of our unique circumstances with my husband's debilitating nerve disease in his arms.

In that passage, the children of Israel were battling with their enemies the Amalekites. Moses told Joshua, the captain of the army, to choose some men to go out and fight Amalek's army. In the meantime, he would stand on the top of a nearby hill with the staff of God in his hand. So Joshua and his men fought with the Amalekites while Moses, his brother Aaron, and a faithful man named Hur went up to the top of the hill. The three men looked over the battle from the top of the hill, and whenever Moses held up his hand, Joshua's army prevailed. But Moses got tired. When he lowered his hands, Amalek's side would start to win. So they got a stone for Moses to sit on, and Aaron and Hur held Moses's arms up steady for the rest of the day. And God's people were victorious over their enemies.

We get weary just like Moses did. As I am writing this, my lower back is kind of achy, and I can feel an unwelcome pressure building in my sinuses again for the third time this winter. Because of my husband's nerve disease in his arms, he experiences chronic pain and needs literal physical help with the things he needs to do with his arms. As a result, we are more consciously aware of how strategic it was for the Lord to create us with two arms! In this awareness, I pray every day for God to provide the arms we need to do whatever it is that he's called us to do. I can testify that God does provide—he does! Even this weekend I have a hard time counting the number of arms that have reached out to help us. A kind man carried my baby's stroller up a flight of stairs at a place where there were no ramps. A sweet university girl came over to help me with homeschooling. Praise God for the Aarons and Hurs among us who are ready to serve.

Regardless of however strong you feel right now, we all need an Aaron and a Hur to hold up our arms when we're weary. We need Aarons and Hurs around us to remind us of how the Son of Man climbed to the top of a hill and held his own arms outstretched on a cross for our salvation. Jesus stayed on that cross until he drank the last drop from the cup of God's wrath against our sin. Jesus was victorious over sin, and now he hands his victory over to us. By faith he gives us his righteousness, and by faith he is the one who lifts our drooping hands to do good works to his glory. Hebrews 12:12–14 says some things about how we can persevere by God's grace in a sin-ridden world:

> Therefore lift your drooping hands and strengthen your weak knees, and make straight paths for your feet, so that what is lame may not be put out of joint but rather be healed. Strive for peace with everyone, and for the holiness without which no one will see the Lord.

Is there something God has called you to do? He can provide you with whatever you need to lift your drooping hands to do it! Is there somewhere you need to strengthen your weak knees and go, for Jesus's sake? God is able to sustain you as you are going. Do you need to turn aside from the path you've been on to walk in holiness instead? God is gracious and ready to forgive.

The text says that we need to strive for peace and holiness. Peace between you and that estranged friend who you've been avoiding is not just going to spontaneously happen. You must pursue it. The fruit of the Holy Spirit isn't going to just spring up inside you without watering the seeds of the gospel that have been sown. God causes the growth, to be sure, but you must cultivate good soil that is ready to receive his Word. By God's grace, do what you need to do to read God's Word and to go to your heavenly Father in prayer. Get the weeds out of your heart, even if the roots are stuck and seem like they won't relent. When another weed shoots up in another place, don't give up. Find an Aaron and a Hur to help you. Surround yourself with friends who will encourage you to look to Christ to give you victory in the battles over the sin inside you.

We want to be among those who "see the Lord"! Every effort we make to pursue holiness must flow from dependence in the grace of God. It is God's grace shown to us on the cross that guarantees grace for our future. He provides!

Look Backward, Look Forward

Consider what Romans 5:1–5 says about how our faith looks back to the cross and forward to eternity and gives cause for rejoicing today:

> Therefore, since we have been justified by faith, we have peace with God through our Lord Jesus Christ. Through him we have also obtained access by faith into this grace in which we stand, and we rejoice in hope of the glory of God. Not only that, but we rejoice in our sufferings, knowing that suffering produces endurance, and endurance produces character, and character produces hope, and hope does not put us to shame, because God's love has been poured into our hearts through the Holy Spirit who has been given to us. (Rom. 5:1–5)

Because of Christ's sacrificial death on the cross we are justified, and we have peace with God today. We stand in grace—that is our permanent, unalterable circumstance. We rejoice in hope of future glory—which is another permanent, unalterable circumstance. Today we stand in grace, and today we rejoice in hope.

The gospel makes the trials I experience good news, because

the indwelling Holy Spirit uses them to produce his fruits of faithful endurance, godly character, and courageous hope.

Milton Vincent's prose on this subject has served my soul immensely. The encouragement came in the middle of the most difficult trial our marriage had faced yet. We had just moved to the Middle East, in the thick of culture shock and language learning, and my husband's physical pain was at an all-time high. Every day it seemed like our circumstances were getting worse and worse. At that pace we were certain that we would soon be destroyed, both spiritually and emotionally. None of the plans we had made were working out, we weren't certain where we would live in a few weeks, I was three years' pregnant with our second child (actually, I was only nine months' pregnant, but at that point it felt like three years), and the church-planting venture was far more difficult than we had ever imagined. On top of all that, my husband's chronic pain was back and worse than ever, and the culture stress of daily life was near maddening. We felt hopeless. On a few occasions I remember trying to lift our empty suitcases out of the cabinet in case we needed to start packing them to leave. We struggled with the idea that our dismal earthly circumstances were the end of the line for us.

Thankfully some friends of ours had loaned us their copy of Vincent's book, and this paragraph changed how we viewed everything:

> The gospel is the one great permanent circumstance in which I live and move; and every hardship in my life is allowed by God only because it serves His gospel purposes in me. When I view my circumstances in this light, I realize that the gospel is not just one piece of good news that fits into my life somewhere among all the bad. I realize instead that the gospel makes genuinely good news out of every other aspect of my life, including my severest trials. The good news about my trials is that God is forcing them to bow to His gospel purposes and do good unto me by improving my character and making me more conformed to the image of Christ.[1]

This isn't just your shallow "the glass is half full, so enjoy what you do have" optimism. This is a declaration of dependence on Christ in all things for the sake of his glory. Believing God's good intentions toward us in making us more like his Son made all the difference. It changed how we responded when the water truck failed to deliver water to our house for the fourth day in a row. It changed how I spoke to my husband when I thought I couldn't bear to hear him say one more time how he was in excruciating pain. It changed my anxious thoughts about our living situation and turned it into an opportunity to see God's hand at work in my life.

Looking to Jesus, Run!

Treasuring Christ changes us. Faith looks back at the cross and agrees with Jesus who said, "It is finished." My debt has been paid and my sin is forgiven because Jesus paid it all. I am reconciled to God through the death of his Son. Faith also looks forward to the future and banks on all that Christ will do for us. Now that we have been reconciled, how much more shall we be saved by his life (Rom. 5:10).

When we see and savor Jesus as our ultimate treasure and are confident in the promises that he has purchased for us with his blood, our faith *works*. This faith in what Christ has done on the cross and faith in what Christ will do for me in the future produces a different Gloria *today* (and a different Hyun Joo, Kasey, Nastaran, Laurie, Amal, Samantha, Priya, Michelle, Bronwyn, Sarah, *and you!*).

Living in the reality of this gospel motivates me to persevere like Jesus did—with resolute joy.

> Therefore, since we are surrounded by so great a cloud of witnesses, let us also lay aside every weight, and sin which clings so closely, and let us run with endurance the race that is set before us, looking to Jesus, the founder and perfecter of our faith, who for the joy that was set before him endured the cross, despising the shame, and is seated at the right hand of the throne of God. Consider him who endured from sinners such hostility against himself, so that you may not grow weary or fainthearted. (Heb. 12:1–3)

So here I am and it's 5 a.m. again. The sun is breaking through the cracks in between the curtains, and I'm so exhausted I can hardly think straight. I'm ready to look to Jesus and consider what he has done and will do when I grow weary or fainthearted. And whatever time it is wherever you are, he can meet you there too.

What a miracle that God would take sinners such as ourselves and give us new hearts with a disposition to love him and trust him in the midst of our circumstances. Self-centered pity is conquered. Faithfulness is produced. This is the supernatural work of a loving God as he meets us in the laundry room, in line at the grocery store, or wherever we are. Praise God for the lovingkindness he's shown us through Jesus.

> Oh, magnify the LORD with me,
>   and let us exalt his name together!
> I sought the LORD , and he answered me
>   and delivered me from all my fears.
> Those who look to him are radiant,
>   and their faces shall never be ashamed.
> This poor man cried, and the LORD heard him
>   and saved him out of all his troubles.
> The angel of the LORD encamps
>   around those who fear him, and delivers them.
> Oh, taste and see that the LORD is good!
>   Blessed is the man who takes refuge in him! (Ps. 34:3–8)

6

The Bread of Life and Bagels for Breakfast

I am constantly amazed by how much of my thought life is consumed with food. My day is organized around food. My budget is adjusted to accommodate food. I finish breakfast and begin thinking about what to feed my kids for lunch. I have cravings for food. I see the food other people are eating, and I have opinions about it. I plan conversations around shared food.

Food is so personal. God created our bodies to both need food and enjoy food. Food is both a life-sustaining necessity and a pleasure.

In our family we all have quirks and preferences regarding which foods we like and don't like. My husband refuses to eat eggs and fish. The girls beg for sprinkles and frosting. I'm a fairly picky eater as well. The one exception to our family food quirks is our son, whose nickname at mealtimes is *Maaz* (the Arabic word for goat).

The Bible teaches that food isn't just a source of calories or temporal satisfaction. God made food such an integral part of our everyday lives so that we would have an idea of what Jesus meant when he said, "I am the bread of life."

Bread from Heaven

God fed the Israelites with manna when they wandered in the wilderness. Manna was what they called the bread that came down from heaven each day. The word *manna* means "What is it?" I was joking with my husband about how frequently I hear this question at mealtime. But it's not because the things I create over the stove are miraculous!

When the Israelites woke up each morning, the manna would be like dew on the ground, and they collected it and prepared it for the day. If they gathered more than they needed, it would rot. God was teaching them to trust him for their daily bread.

In John 6 Jesus is talking with a crowd that had gathered as they looked for him. Jesus had just fed a crowd of thousands of people with only a few loaves of bread and a few fish. The people wanted another miracle. They wanted to be fed. Jesus said to them, "Truly, truly, I say to you, you are seeking me, not because you saw signs, but because you ate your fill of the loaves" (John 6:26).

But the crowd didn't know that Jesus had more for them than bread that would only satisfy their hunger for a few hours. "Do not work for the food that perishes, but for the food that endures to eternal life, which the Son of Man will give to you. For on him God the Father has set his seal" (v. 27).

"What must we do, to be doing the works of God?" the crowd asked Jesus. Jesus answered them, "This is the work of God, that you believe in him whom he has sent" (vv. 28–29). Then the crowd asked a potentially saucy follow-up question: God gave us manna to eat, so what are *you* going to give us? So Jesus tells them:

> Truly, truly, I say to you, it was not Moses who gave you the bread from heaven, but my Father gives you the true bread from heaven. For the bread of God is he who comes down from heaven and gives life to the world. . . . I am the bread of life; whoever comes to me shall not hunger, and whoever believes in me shall never thirst. . . . Truly, truly, I say to you, whoever believes has eternal life. I am the bread of life. Your fathers ate the manna in the wilderness, and they died. This is the bread that comes down from heaven, so that one may eat of it and not die. I am the living bread that came down from heaven. If anyone eats of this bread, he will live forever. And the bread that I will give for the life of the world is my flesh. (vv. 32–33, 35, 47–51)

Jesus said that the manna in the wilderness was pointing to him. The manna came down from heaven; Jesus came down from heaven. The Father sent the manna; the Father sent Jesus.

The manna gave life to the Israelites; Jesus gives life to the world. The manna gave life for a little while; Jesus is the living bread who gives eternal life through the sacrifice of his own body on the cross.

Jesus is saying that the cost of bread in God's kingdom is just to be hungry for it. He's given us his body so that we can work for what satisfies us eternally. The work of God, Jesus says, is to "believe in him whom he has sent" (v. 29). This passage echoes Isaiah's prophecy,

> Come, everyone who thirsts,
>   come to the waters;
> and he who has no money,
>   come, buy and eat!
> Come, buy wine and milk
>   without money and without price.
> Why do you spend your money for that which is not bread,
>   and your labor for that which does not satisfy?
> Listen diligently to me, and eat what is good,
>   and delight yourselves in rich food.
> Incline your ear, and come to me;
>   hear, that your soul may live;
> and I will make with you an everlasting covenant,
>   my steadfast, sure love for David. (Isa. 55:1–3)

This is a great truth to meditate on next time you hear your stomach rumbling for food. Before you head to the kitchen, take a moment to remember how the bread of life came down from heaven and gave his life so that sinners could be reconciled to God and be satisfied in him forever.

Freedom from Food-Borne Sin

God created food for his purposes, but food can be a source of so much anxiety and conflict. Some people fight over dwindling food supplies, while others have fisticuff arguments over which icing should decorate their wedding cake. Just the other day I witnessed a disagreement between a waiter and a customer over whether the coffee he served her was a cappuccino or a latte.

We get so worked up about what meals to make for our families or guests, over the rising prices of the food we buy, the dishes we envisioned but couldn't create, and the feedback we receive for the food we've served.

"What's for supper?" "What's in this?" "There isn't any more?" "How many calories is that?" "What did this cost?" These simple food-related questions have the power to stir up so many emotions in us. Often the prevailing emotion is anxiety. If left unchecked, anxiety gives rise to unbelief and a host of other problems that bleed out into other areas of our lives. As homemakers we're tempted to devote ourselves to building our identity out of what we put on the dinner table. We're tempted to revel in people-pleasing. We're tempted to compare ourselves to others. We're tempted to feed our superior attitudes about our taste in food. All this for *food*!

How easy it is to obsess over food and miss the point of food. The purpose of planning meals, shopping for groceries, cooking, and serving food is to get your spiritual appetite rumbling for God's superiority in all things. God is infinitely superior to the food he created to sustain the bodies he's given us for the purpose of glorifying him in all things.

God has given us his Son, and when we believe in him, we can be free from the sin that so easily entangles us. Jesus, through the gospel, frees us. We can be free from judging others by what they are able to create in the kitchen. We can be free from criticizing others for what they feed their families. We can be free from comparing ourselves to models of culinary perfection. We can be free from eating the bread of anxious toil. We can be free from feeling insecure about what we are not able to create in the kitchen. We can be free to give away what we have, because we have a better possession in Christ. When we live in the reality of our identity in Christ, we discover we are free.

A Very Thin List of Things to Worry About

Food is one of the things that we like to worry about. It's interesting how in Matthew 6:25 Jesus makes a list of things we shouldn't be anxious about, and he includes food:

> Therefore I tell you, do not be anxious about your life, what you will eat or what you will drink, nor about your body, what you will put on. Is not life more than food, and the body more than clothing?

One can hardly think of a more comprehensive list of potential worries: life, food, drink, body, and clothes.

Jesus wisely knows that people who worry like to compare themselves to others. So he gives us a comparison chart. In the next verses Jesus puts our anxiety into more explicit perspective when he compares us to birds, lilies, and grass:

> Look at the birds of the air; they neither sow nor reap nor gather into barns, and yet your heavenly Father feeds them. Are you not of more value than they? And which of you by being anxious can add a single hour to his span of life? And why are you anxious about clothing? Consider the lilies of the field, how they grow; they neither toil nor spin, yet I tell you, even Solomon in all his glory was not arrayed like one of these. But if God so clothes the grass of the field, which today is alive and tomorrow is thrown into the oven, will he not much more clothe you, O you of little faith? (Matt. 6:26–30)

God is not unaware of our propensity to worry and chase after temporary fixes. God is not oblivious to how difficult it is for us to believe that he is our all-satisfying treasure, that Jesus is our bread of life. God loves us, he has immeasurable grace for us because of Christ (Eph. 4:7), and he is ready to bear our burdens because he cares for us. "Humble yourselves, therefore, under the mighty hand of God so that at the proper time he may exalt you, casting all your anxieties on him, because he cares for you" (1 Pet. 5:6–7).

Anxiousness and Futility Are Like Cousins

I know it is so easy to feel futile when we consider the magnitude of the worries that are on our minds. The burden of complicated circumstances can make us feel paralyzed, and naturally we want a way out.

I know it's easy to settle for pacifiers instead of the peace of Christ that passes all understanding. It's like the chips trick at Mexican restaurants. They bring you this gigantic basket of bottomless tortilla chips while you peruse the menu. You make your selection, tell it to your waiter, and while you're waiting for your meal you fill up on chips. You've made peace with your stomach temporarily at the cost of a good meal that you can't fully enjoy because your belly hurts from eating all the chips.

My kids cry out for things like this all the time when meals aren't coming fast enough for them. They beg for cereal and milk when there's a chicken roasting in the oven. They need to be patient and wait.

We have a problem with letting God provide for us. We have a problem with that in the broad scope of our lives—we'd rather save ourselves from our sin. And we have a problem with letting God provide for our daily bread in the minute details of life. We fail at letting God provide for us because we think we know what we need better than he does. So we go and take it for ourselves. I do this every time I don't consciously trust him; I trust myself.

I need hope. I'm all too familiar with the gut-queasy feeling that goes along with the sentiment, "Oh no, I've blown it." But God is greater, more powerful, and more mysterious than we could ever dream, and it will take an eternity for him to reveal to us his magnificence.

Feeling futile over our inability to trust God when we're anxious should not be a source of despair. This is an occasion to worship! How great is God, who is so desirable and worthy of our worship that our hearts must feel empty when we know we're not full of his joy! How merciful is Jesus, who gave us his righteousness and bears away our sin! If you have any sorrow, if you experience any reluctance over your hardness of heart, do not be discouraged. You would not feel that way if the Spirit of God were not at work in your life. If you were left to your own devices, then there would be no need to feel like kicking yourself because you know you're missing out on seeing and savoring God.

Feeling like you want to kick yourself for a waning appetite for God is a grace to you. People who truly don't desire God *don't* desire God. Richard Sibbes explained this in *The Tender Heart*:

> But the child of God has not total and final hardness of heart, but has a sensibleness of it, he feels and sees it. Total hardness feels nothing, but a Christian that has hardness of heart, feels that he has it; as a man that has the stone in his bladder, feels and knows that he has a stone. A hard-hearted man feels nothing, but he that has but only hardness of heart does feel: for there is a difference between hardness of heart and a hard heart; for the child of God may have *hardness of heart*, but not a *hard heart*.[1]

So don't be anxious when you obviously display an appetite for more of God. He will surely give you more of himself when the desire of your heart is for him. "Delight yourself in the LORD, and he will give you the desires of your heart" (Ps. 37:4).

The Lord's Prayer Sung at a Fountain

One chilly desert night my husband and I were on a date at a shopping mall. There were singing fountains at this mall. These fountains were synchronized to play according to selected songs. Each night starting at 7 p.m. these songs would play through the speakers around the fountain, and the water show would happen every half hour or so. Only a few select songs were in the rotation. There were songs from different genres of music—an Arabic song, a famous Bollywood song, and a Celine Dion song or two, plus a selection from an opera.

On this particular night there was a song I had never heard before, but it sounded vaguely familiar. The hauntingly beautiful melody echoed from the speakers—the lyrics were Swahili. I recognized the phrase "*Baba yetu*" and a few other Swahili words from the brief time we had spent in Kenya. This song was the Lord's Prayer, sung by a Swahili choir. The fountains danced as the choir was singing of the glories of our Father God, who provides everything we need for life and godliness through his Son Jesus Christ.

A chill went up my spine. I couldn't believe what I was hearing and the place in which I was hearing it. These were Jesus's ancient words that have been proclaimed to generations and generations of people who would hear with their ears and see with their hearts that Jesus is the ultimate answer to that very prayer.

God our Father is holy, holy, holy, and he is worthy of our worship. But we can't hallow his name, because we are utterly sinful. Jesus did the Father's will perfectly in his life and in his death. Jesus is our daily bread, as he declared himself to be the bread of life. Through Jesus we are forgiven, and through Jesus we can forgive others who sin against us. Jesus was led into temptation, yet he conquered sin. When we are tempted to sin, then Jesus gives us his strength to choose joy and life in him instead. Jesus leads us into righteousness and life eternal—not into temptation. Jesus delivers us from evil and will finally swallow up evil forever.

Jesus is the ultimate answer to the Lord's Prayer.

My heart wanted to explode right there as I leaned on the iron fence surrounding that fountain. I felt like wailing and dancing at the same time. How could such a magnificent truth be entrusted to people like us to neglect it and forget about it and spurn it? How could the God who indwells us with his Holy Spirit be so patient? How could he desire that we not perish? How great is our

God who gives us a hope that will not fail or put us to shame as he pours his love into our hearts through the Holy Spirit *who has been given to us* (Rom. 5:5)?

I looked over my shoulder at this crowd of at least a thousand souls hailing from nations across the globe. The Lord brought this passage in Isaiah to mind:

> On this mountain the LORD of hosts will make for all peoples
>> a feast of rich food, a feast of well-aged wine,
>> of rich food full of marrow, of aged wine well refined.
> And he will swallow up on this mountain
>> the covering that is cast over all peoples,
>> the veil that is spread over all nations.
> He will swallow up death forever;
> and the Lord GOD will wipe away tears from all faces,
>> and the reproach of his people he will take away from all
>>> the earth,
>> for the LORD has spoken.
> It will be said on that day,
>> "Behold, this is our God; we have waited for him, that he
>>> might save us.
>> This is the LORD; we have waited for him;
>> let us be glad and rejoice in his salvation." (Isa. 25:6–9)

Jesus is the hope of the nations! Yet so many people don't wait for his salvation. We die trying to save ourselves. As I watched and listened to the singing fountains, tears slid down my cheeks and were caught by the wind. The emotion I felt that night was a shadow of what Jesus felt as he looked out over a crowd once and said he was moved deeply because the people were like sheep without a shepherd.

He Cares for You—Trust Him!

This Jesus who tells us not to be anxious for anything is the Son of God who has been given charge over all things in the universe. Surely a mother loves her child who dotes on that child and has memorized every birthmark and personality quirk of that child.

How much more does the God who knows the number of hairs on your head love you and care for what you need?

Jesus was pleased to die in our place. He justified the ungodly and gave us his righteousness. No one took Jesus's life; he laid it down himself: "No one takes it from me, but I lay it down of my own accord. I have authority to lay it down, and I have authority to take it up again. This charge I have received from my Father" (John 10:18).

Would you look to Jesus to lead you? "For the Lamb in the midst of the throne will be their shepherd, and he will guide them to springs of living water, and God will wipe away every tear from their eyes" (Rev. 7:17).

Plead with your own soul the glories of Jesus and be glad in him and rejoice in his salvation! Trust him with the anxieties of your heart because he cares for you! Wrestle your rebellious heart into submission of his lovingkindness if you have to. Jesus is the great shepherd, and he is the only one who can guide you to springs of living water.

Zealous Homemaking for Jesus

The Bible is clear on our purpose, our problem, our peace, and our portion. We were created in God's image to nurture others, but we've fallen to sinful self-centeredness. We fail to worship God as we ought through obeying him. But God! God sent Christ our redeemer to be our peace by atoning for our sin and giving us his righteousness. Now in Jesus, the bread of life, we have an inheritance that will never fade away.

Keeping a home, serving strangers, "settling down," raising a family—none of this was ever about us. It was always for the sake of the gospel. I have to constantly remind myself of this, so I've memorized Titus 2:11–14, which is the impetus for the oft-quoted Titus 2:3–5:

> Older women likewise are to be reverent in behavior, not slander-
> ers or slaves to much wine. They are to teach what is good, and

so train the young women to love their husbands and children, to be self-controlled, pure, working at home, kind, and submissive to their own husbands, that the word of God may not be reviled.

Titus 2:3–5 is a description of how Christian women ought to behave, and it gives the reason why: so that the Word of God may not be reviled. In other words, we conduct ourselves in this manner so that our behavior affirms, not contradicts, the message of the gospel. Titus 2:11–14 expands on the *why* behind all of these instructions:

> For the grace of God has appeared, bringing salvation for all people, training us to renounce ungodliness and worldly passions, and to live self-controlled, upright, and godly lives in the present age, waiting for our blessed hope, the appearing of the glory of our great God and Savior Jesus Christ, who gave himself for us to redeem us from all lawlessness and to purify for himself a people for his own possession who are zealous for good works. (Titus 2:11–14)

What a high calling and privilege it is to be a zealous homemaker for Jesus! So in your homemaking, cooking, wifery, kid raising, and hospitality, feast your soul on the bread of life and do whatever you need to do in order to help people yearn for the true bread that gives life.

7

All Grace and All Sufficiency for Every Dinner Guest

I like to think of myself as an easygoing person, especially when it comes to sharing. I like to think that I'm happy to give whatever I have if it means it will help someone. "Sharing is caring!" my South African friends like to say, and I like to think that truism is embodied in my laissez-faire attitude about sharing a kitchen with the church.

The Great Coffee-Filter Conundrum

Yes, I share a kitchen with our church. Our home functions sort of like a parsonage-slash-church office-slash-meeting space. Every family needs a kitchen, every office needs a kitchen, and every meeting space needs a kitchen. All three of these entities use the same kitchen, but thankfully, by God's grace, there are three refrigerators in that one kitchen!

I usually don't mind the occasional "Where did this or that dish and spoon run off to?" I honestly don't. But even with my easygoing attitude, sharing a kitchen has been a challenge for me. I would even say that sharing things (in general) has been a venue for sanctification in my life. Isn't that just like the Lord to use things that are so common to us to shape our souls and make us more ready for eternal life in heaven?

The first thing I look for in the kitchen in the mornings are coffee filters. I drink coffee every morning.

I even like to give the morning a name depending on the kind of coffee I'll require to manage it. If the children sleep past 7 a.m. and emerge from their pristine rooms with big smiles on their faces all dressed and holding hands, then it's just an Americano kind of morning. If I have lost the last half-hour of sleep I had hoped for, and the baby fussed through my morning devotional time, which I hastily finish when I discover that the rank smell coming through the air vents is someone's leaking diarrhea diaper, then I call that a double-shot-of-espresso-with-no-sense-of-humor kind of morning.

The Great Coffee Filter Conundrum in question happened on just an ordinary morning. It was a watered-down-iced-coffee kind of day. In order to make said iced coffee I needed some fresh brew to start with. And in order to brew some coffee I needed a coffee filter, the last of which had been taken and used by the group that used the meeting rooms the night before. I'd be lying if I said I wasn't frustrated. Why did they have to go into my cupboard and take my last coffee filter?

Coffee Filters Are the Least of My Concerns

The second after I felt that twinge of entitlement, I realized how petty it all was. Really—what does a cup of iced coffee mean in the scope of eternity? My life is hidden in Christ, and that should give me cause for an eternity of joy. Didn't Jesus say that life is more than the body, and the body is more than food? Surely coffee falls into that category, right? If I know all these things, then why can't I gladly share something as insignificant as a coffee filter to make others glad?

Clearly, the problem is with me. That incident clearly told me that no matter how easygoing I think I am, I have an acute sense of entitlement. Something as insignificant as a coffee filter, which weighs less than a gram, can load the burden of the entire law of God on my shoulders. In that singular spark of angry entitlement I was guilty of offending the holiness of God. I need a Savior!

In his famous Sermon on the Mount, Jesus said, "You have heard that it was said to those of old, 'You shall not murder; and whoever murders will be liable to judgment.' But I say to you that everyone who is angry with his brother will be liable to judgment; whoever insults his brother will be liable to the council; and whoever says, 'You fool!' will be liable to the hell of fire" (Matt. 5:21–22). It may seem like an overreaction to have my anger compared to murder. But Jesus is clear—unrighteous anger is a sin against God. Although the consequences of these two sins are different, Jesus's point is that all our sin is against a God who is infinitely holy. Murder is an attempt to blot out the image of God here on earth. Unrighteous anger against someone made in the image of God is an offense to the Creator. When we minimize the offensiveness of our sin, we are attempting to diminish the holiness of God.

My outburst of anger is but one aspect of my offense. The selfishness that motivated the anger is also a mark against me. The attitude of superiority over other people is another. And so is the prideful assumption that I am the best sharer in the world. The case against me keeps stacking up, and no lawyer can find a loophole in God's perfect law to acquit me of these crimes against his holiness.

What am I to do the next time something of mine is taken, used, requested, or given? Believe the good news! The Judge himself has put forward his own Son to bear the punishment for my sin and give to me his own perfect righteousness. I will be free from this entangling sin only to the degree that I have repented of it and joyfully rest in the saving work of Christ instead. Only Jesus can replace the desire I have to dictate how and when and if my possessions are shared with others.

I Can't Give

I know this desire to dictate how and when and if my possessions are shared with others doesn't stop in my coffee cabinet. It doesn't stop in my kitchen either. It extends to every aspect of my home, my pocketbook, my family, my time, and my life. The tendrils of the vine of greed and pride and selfishness wrap themselves around my heart.

Not that I don't have anything to give to others—I can surely afford to donate a dozen packages of coffee filters. I have the resources to open my kitchen to anyone who wants to use it. We have space in our villa to loan to anyone who has need of it any morning, afternoon, or evening. I have twenty-four hours every day that are available to those who need me. The issue isn't with the resources I have; the issue lies with my willingness to share them and where these resources come from.

If I forever try to extend hospitality to others using only the insufficient and limited kindness resident in my heart, then I feel sorry for anyone who ever sits at my kitchen table or lays his head on the pillows in our guest room. If the hospitality I give to others comes only from what I have to offer, then my guests are better off sleeping outside the gate.

Jesus Is the True and Better Host

I might try a number of strategies to fix my greed/pride/selfishness problem, but true repentance is elusive in my self-motivated strategies to become a more hospitable person. So what can effect lasting change in my heart? God's kindness is meant to lead us to repentance (Rom. 2:4). There is a God-directed thankfulness that is a durable gratitude in the face of want and need. When grief over our sin and thankfulness for the gift of grace meet together at the cross, a powerful work of transformation occurs in our hearts. If we know we are already saved by the work that Christ has done on the cross, we can have gutsy confidence in Christ to cheerfully, sacrificially give to others. When we behold the promises of God in Christ by faith, we repent of our sin and rejoice in Jesus!

Jesus is the true and better host, who calls us into God's very presence through the sacrifice of his own body. Christ our Lord gives us the greatest picture of hospitality that the world has ever seen. Jesus gave his life so we could be guaranteed a place in his Father's house forever. He defeated the darkness so we could live in the city that is lit by the light of the Lamb. Now, that's biblical hospitality! Because of Christ's sacrificial death on the cross, God welcomes us spiritual orphans into his forever family.

But not only is Jesus the epitome of hospitality; he is also our Savior. His record of perfect hospitality is credited to us as we receive his righteousness by faith. His hospitable work on the cross makes it possible for God to forgive our sins. The heavenly hospitality of the holy Trinity is the grandest gesture of selfless-ness, openness, humility, generosity, and love that the world has ever seen. God does open-heart surgery on us so that we can have open homes to his glory.

Think of it: God the Father designed a plan to redeem fallen humanity, restoring us to a right relationship with him, and will eventually glorify us to sinless perfection so that we might wor-ship him for all eternity. God the Son humbled himself in the incarnation and entered into his own creation, taking up residence in a womb he created. In his life he exemplified great humility as he faced our every temptation in order to become our Great High Priest. In his death he humbled himself on the cross and bore our sins as a criminal although he never sinned.

And though we have spurned his perfect witness to the great-ness of God's glory since the fall in the garden of Eden, the Holy Spirit generously continues his ministry of convicting the world of sin, lovingly administers God's common grace, and humbly takes up residence in the hearts of the redeemed children of God. We see through God's hospitality how he is committed to making his glory central in the story of redemption.

Serve with the Strength God Supplies

Knowing how God gives us hospitality in the gospel is not the same as living in the reality of it or being able to extend this hos-pitality to others.

Every effort in hospitality must flow from a dependence on the grace of God—the grace shown to us on the cross that guarantees grace for our future. We look back on the cross and see how Jesus showed us what hospitality looks like in accepting others for God's sake to bring them near to God. And we look forward to grace in Jesus Christ as he also supplies what we need in order to extend gracious hospitality to others.

Because of God's grace in the gospel, our hospitality can be selfless, generous, and authentic. One of the ways we are liberated from pride, greed, and fear in our hospitality is when we serve with the strength God supplies. "Whoever speaks, as one who speaks oracles of God; whoever serves, as one who serves by the strength that God supplies—in order that in everything God may be glorified through Jesus Christ. To him belong glory and dominion forever and ever. Amen" (1 Pet. 4:11).

So how do we serve with the strength God supplies so that he gets the glory? Philippians 4:19 shows us another connection between God's supply and his glory: "And my God will supply every need of yours according to his riches in glory in Christ Jesus." God's supply for our ministry flows from Jesus—a supply that is as limitless as the power of the risen Christ as he sits on his throne.

When we serve with the strength God supplies instead of from our own energies or motivation, we can serve with cheerfulness to the praise of his glory. We don't have to be embittered martyrs on the altar of hospitality.

Don't Paganize Christian Hospitality

D. A. Carson warns us against using hospitality and service as a means to glorify ourselves. "If we take on Christian service, and think of such service as the vehicle that will make us central, we have paganized Christian service; we have domesticated Christian living and set it to servitude in a pagan cause."[1]

Who hasn't been in someone else's home where they felt like the home or the meal was an intentionally orchestrated display to the glory of the host? And who of us hasn't *been* that hostess?

Our craving for admiration is diluted and the praise of others is muffled as we serve with the strength God supplies. Why would we take credit for the fruit of the Holy Spirit in our lives?

Sometimes it's not always clear to my kids what I've put in their meals. My oldest will often ask, "Mommy, what did you put in this smoothie?" or "How did you make my sandwich?" Half the time I like to tease her with an answer like, "It's my new smoothie recipe—unicorn hooves and postage stamps. Why? Do you like it?" Other times I'll tell her that I put cuddles, confidence, and grace in the blender for them, or that I made their sandwiches with peace and love. It sounds silly, but it's a reminder to me that when I feed people I should do so with the love of Christ, with an aim to honor him. Feeding people is more than giving them life-sustaining calories; it's an opportunity to share with them the soul-reviving grace of God.

Serving with the strength God supplies according to his riches in Christ solves the problem we have with self-serving hospitality. When someone comes into our home, we can focus on presenting Jesus instead of on our presentation of ourselves.

Has there ever been a time when we weren't tempted to feel like all we have to offer a guest is what is in our kitchen cabinets? When our souls are filled with the glories of the gospel, we can hold out to our guests the bread of life!

When we consider the generosity of the Son of God in giving his life, we are free to give anything and everything he has given us so that we may know him better.

Every minuscule effort of sharing the gifts God has given us is amplified and multiplied to his praise, just as with the loaves and fish. Our service to others pleases God when it is done for his sake and is an overflow of our faith in him. I've served both water in paper cups and gourmet meals in an elaborate spread while considering the truth that God is well pleased with my work done by faith.

Our excuses for not cheerfully serving in hospitality are legion. We don't have time, we don't have space, there are other people we consider more important, we don't have nice enough things to share, we don't have the ingredients to make the meal we'd prefer to serve, our home isn't much compared to what others have, and on and on. The good news of the gospel frees us from the self-absorbed rationalizations we make that hinder us from extending gracious hospitality toward one another. As our faith ascertains the truthfulness of God's claims to be able to supply our every need, we experience the riches of God's grace in Christ, and he helps us to happily loosen the grip we have on our stuff, our time, and our energy.

The Joy of the Lord Strengthens You for Hospitality

What would our hospitality look like if we believed that Jesus's death on the cross was the measure of God's compassion for someone? Oh, how we would seek to serve them with the strength that God provides!

I've experienced hospitality from people whose hopes were set on God. Their faith in God's provision caused them to be truly generous and ready to share whatever they had with us—even their own bed. Our friends, who were new acquaintances at the time, heard that our family would be traveling back and forth to their city on a regular basis. They were eager to share their apartment with us on those weekends. I remember asking my husband, "But they don't have a spare room, do they?" His reply was simply, "I think they have that figured out." Our new friends cheerfully gave our family their bedroom while they bunked in with their two boys on a foldout couch. Over those weekends, on several occasions our hostess even commented, "What a blessing for us! We love having you here, and we love bunking with our boys!"

We were created in Christ Jesus to walk in good works such as showing hospitality (Eph. 2:10), so we should show hospitality in a manner worthy of God's call. Jesus supplies the agape love we need, and when our souls are satisfied in him, we overflow in love to others. When we love our neighbors in this way, we imitate God and walk in love as Christ has loved us (Eph. 5:1–2). So rejoice in Jesus's provision of love, and watch how love freely flows from your home to bless any whom God brings across your doorstep.

True hospitality cannot be anything but God glorifying. God gets the glory when we serve with the strength he provides.

The righteousness of Christ is our hope, as we've all missed the mark in his standards of perfect, cheerful giving in hospitality. The joy of Christ will also be our comfort and our delight.

In Nehemiah 8, when Ezra the priest read aloud the Book of the Law to God's people all morning long, the conviction of their sin pierced their hearts, and they grieved. Every man, woman, and child was weeping. Actually, they were near hysteria. The text says that Nehemiah, Ezra, and all the Levites (priests) had to repeatedly calm them down. What words would comfort such grieving souls who had seen the holiness of God in his perfect law and compared it with their own sinfulness? Nehemiah 8:10 tells us what Nehemiah said to the people: "Go your way. Eat the fat and drink sweet wine and send portions to anyone who has nothing ready, for this day is holy to our Lord. And do not be grieved, for the joy of the Lord is your strength."

If the joy of the Lord is the strength of the repentant Israelites, it is true for me, a redeemed child of the Most High. God is not content to merely provide the strength we need for hospitality, but he aims to be our delight as we serve others.

We're destined for joy forever because of Christ's exquisite hospitality in opening a way to God through his own body. We can serve others with gladness, knowing that the carrots we peel and the diapers we change are as unto the Lord.

When we show hospitality in this way, we can see how "God is able to make all grace abound to you, so that having all sufficiency in all things at all times, you may abound in every good work" (2 Cor. 9:8). Our role is to serve with the strength God supplies, and it's God's role to do with our service whatever he pleases. He supplies the strength, and in his abundant hospitality he also gives us joy!

An Eternal Perspective on Coffee Filters

God's grace in Christ is for us to enjoy and share with others. When I have this grace in mind, I can see my possessions and others' needs in light of eternity. What's a coffee filter, really? What is it when compared to Jesus, who is my lasting possession in heaven?

When I share my insignificant stuff for Jesus's sake, he says it is significant to him: "And whoever gives one of these little ones even a cup of cold water because he is a disciple, truly, I say to you, he will by no means lose his reward" (Matt. 10:42). Even just a cup of water, when shared for Jesus's sake, is an extension of the hospitality that Jesus showed us on the cross.

In my case it might be even better if that cup of water is heated to boiling and is steeped in ground-up coffee beans. I trust that God can give me the joy in him that I need in order to share that cup, too.

8

He Washes Us
White as Snow

If there were one thing I would change about my home in a moment's notice, it would be my kitchen floor. It is quite possibly the bane of my domestic existence. And for that reason, I'm convinced that God chooses to use my kitchen floor to conform my character to that of Christ by stretching me in the areas of patience, fortitude, and self-control. How could a kitchen floor be the cause of so much consternation and spiritual conflict? Let me explain.

My Disgusting Kitchen Floor

The floor is between ten and fifteen years old. It is white cement tile that has long since lost its protective veneer. The tiles are joined together by deeply grooved white grout. I'm sure in her glory days the floor might have been spectacular—maybe even the pride and joy of the lady of the house. But those days are gone. Oh, are they ever *gone*.

If you so much as walk on said kitchen floor with less-than-pristine feet or shoes, the tiles absorb your dirt like a sponge. When you attempt to sweep up crumbs from your breakfast toast, the bread tumbles down into the grout canyons, luring the ants to trail in for a feast. If someone spills any kind of liquid on the floor (which happens continually throughout the day in our house), then the liquid seeps into the cement grout and reawakens "The Stink." The Stink is the name I've given to the malodorous scent that nobody can quite put a finger on. "What's that smell? Where is it coming from?" It's The Stink. If I could just throw money at the problem and pay someone to renovate the kitchen, I would do it yesterday.

I can say with confidence that I have tried every cleaning product available to me. I've had the grout "built up" so that it isn't nearly as deep as it was before—twice. I've even considered getting a puppy dog for the express purpose of letting the puppy eat the food that drops on the kitchen floor. That would solve the ant problem. Playing with puppies is more fun than scrubbing with bleach. But alas, puppies come with their own messes, and nobody in our house is jumping to make it their job to clean up after a puppy.

"Who would build a kitchen with bright white cement tiles!" my husband sympathizes with me.

He's right—who would choose such a hard-to-clean element for the room in your home that gets filthy several times a day?

The only thing that comes remotely close to being effective in removing the dirt from the kitchen floor is a pressurized air blower. Unfortunately, pressurized air blowers are not cost effective or practical. Otherwise I would use one to get the junk off my kitchen floor after each meal.

The cleaning products all promise the same thing—100 percent guaranteed to clean 99.9 percent of the bacteria and grime. And they all fail to deliver. The floor will never be perfectly clean, and the sand and food is just going to keep coming. I'll just have to settle for "as clean as it's ever going to get" or turn it into a beach and be done pretending that I can clean it.

Heart, We Have a Problem

My disgusting kitchen floor and its propensity to absorb filth is a picture of our hearts. No matter how hard we scrub, we cannot erase our iniquity. The shame of our sin is like the phantom stain on a shirt that reappears after you've dried it. The stain is deep in the fibers of the shirt, and when the right temperature of heat is applied, the stain rises to the surface of the fabric. The stain is permanent.

King David acutely felt his need to be cleansed of his sin. After Nathan the prophet confronted him for adultery, murder, and lying, David wrote Psalm 51. In verses 1–2 he wrote:

> Have mercy on me, O God,
>   according to your steadfast love;
> according to your abundant mercy
>   blot out my transgressions.
> Wash me thoroughly from my iniquity,
>   and cleanse me from my sin!

David's sins were grievous and had far-reaching consequences for himself, the family he destroyed, and his kingdom. Sometimes we read about his affair with Bathsheba and the murder of her husband and feel we can't relate. We might think in our hearts that adultery and conspiracy to commit murder just don't seem relevant to our relative morality. We like to believe that we would be like David when he is slaying the giant Goliath. But when it comes to this aspect of David's life we like to imagine that we are more like Nathan.

But what David says in verses 4 and 5 ends arguments of self-justification right in their tracks:

> Against you, you only, have I sinned
>   and done what is evil in your sight,
> so that you may be justified in your words
>   and blameless in your judgment.
> Behold, I was brought forth in iniquity,
>   and in sin did my mother conceive me.

David seduced Bathsheba and murdered her husband, yet he says that his sin is against God. David says that not only did he do something that God considers evil, but that he himself is evil: "I was brought forth in iniquity." As King David is, so are we all—we *are* sinners who *do* sins.

As much as I dislike my kitchen floor, I can appreciate how looking at the floor gives me an occasion to remember the gospel. My dingy kitchen floor problem is not so different from the problem of sin. Our methods for getting rid of the stain of sin on our hearts are ineffective. We sweep our guilt aside into another place and bury it in crevices of our hearts. But then the next time something spills into the crevices, The Stink fills our nostrils, and we wonder, "Where's that coming from?"

I used to think that I had a long fuse when it came to my propensity to get angry with people. "Oh, I am so patient," I would tell myself. "I can go for great lengths of time without getting angry at anyone!" Then when I finally got angry, it would be explosive. Sharp words would fly like daggers through the air to pierce the hearts of anyone in earshot. Was I really so patient after all? No, I was sweeping aside my bitterness to feed my anger. I wasn't killing anger by severing it at the root by forgiving people. When the opportunity would arise to finally express how I felt, it became obvious that The Stink in my heart was alive and thriving. I pity the fool who gets in this fool's way when she's mad.

The Stink in our hearts affecting other people is not our biggest problem. We are inefficient in dealing with our sin and the consequences of our sin, such as guilt and death, but our sin foremost offends God. God is pure and holy. "Though you wash yourself with lye and use much soap, the stain of your guilt is still before me, declares the Lord God" (Jer. 2:22).

Job described God's righteous fury with sin despite his attempts to cleanse his guilt:

> If I wash myself with snow
>   and cleanse my hands with lye,
> yet you will plunge me into a pit,
>   and my own clothes will abhor me.
> For he is not a man, as I am, that I might answer him,
>   that we should come to trial together.
> There is no arbiter between us,
>   who might lay his hand on us both. (Job 9:30–33)

Job lamented that reconciliation with God is not possible because of the great gulf between God and man. God is wholly other—he is creator and we are his creation. Job was right in saying that no man can intercede on another man's behalf before God's holy throne.

That is why the incarnation of the eternal Son of God is so spectacular. That the Holy Spirit would conceive the Son of God in Mary's womb as part of God's plan to save his people is astonishing. Only Jesus the God-man could be the arbiter between God and man. There is a redeemer, and he's the only one who can deal effectively with our sin and guilt.

She Hit Me First!

Maybe you don't sense the need for cleansing from your sin. Perhaps you feel like you've worked hard on eliminating the gross sins in your life to make yourself "as clean as you're ever going to get." Or perhaps you feel that enough time has gone by to wipe out your sin because the bigger consequences seem to have gone away. I understand that.

Many of us struggle to identify with David's prayer in Psalm 51, because his sins had catastrophic results, and we can't see how anything we've ever done is as reprehensible as what he did. We commit a critical error when we do this. When we compare our sins to someone else's—anyone else's—we are measuring our righteousness to that of our neighbors. We do this without even thinking. Nobody had to teach our preschooler to say, "But she hit me first!" to try to absolve herself of guilt in a sibling squabble. When we get older we say, "At least I'm not like that grievous sinner over there." We echo the Pharisee, "God, I thank you that I am not like other men, extortioners, unjust, adulterers, or even like this tax collector" (Luke 18:11).

This is exactly why Psalm 51:4 is so instructive for us. David says to God, "Against you, you only, have I sinned and done what is evil in your sight, so that you may be justified in your words and blameless in your judgment." It is no difficult thing to justify yourself by comparing your deeds and sins to those of someone else.

But the Bible says of humanity, "Every intention of the thoughts of his heart [is] only evil continually" (Gen. 6:5). When the apostle Peter rebuked a magician who wanted to abuse the power of God to make money, he pointed out the connection between the magician's sin and his heart: "Repent, therefore, of this wickedness of yours, and pray to the Lord that, if possible, the intent of your heart may be forgiven you" (Acts 8:22).

We're sinners not only in what we do but also in what we *don't* do. The Bible says that we "do evil" when we do not set our hearts to seek the Lord (2 Chron. 12:14).

Listen to Your Mouth

One of the most common ways that the Holy Spirit convinces me of my sinfulness and my need for the purifying power of God in my life is through what I say. Not a day goes by when I don't feel like kicking myself over something stupid I've said to someone in person, on the phone, or to the whole world of "friends" and "followers" in a social media context.

Take yesterday, for example. I was talking with a friend, and I said something sarcastic that I could tell probably offended her. It was so dumb that it isn't even worth repeating so that its dumbness lives on in your mind too. I even heaped more insult onto God's glory when, out of sheer laziness and pride, I made no effort to clarify, explain, or apologize to her.

To further illumine my need for a Savior, when I felt conviction from God about my careless words, I justified them. "*She* shouldn't be so sensitive," I reasoned. Not only did I err in what I said, but I erred in how I said it and what I didn't say afterward. When initially confronted with my offense against God, I threw the blame onto my friend. I offended God, who created me to the praise of his glory. Here I was choosing to worship myself instead.

I also offended my neighbor, one who was made in the image of God to reflect his glory.

Clearly I am a sinner. Clearly I need God's purifying power to rescue me from my sin and empower me to say things that are good, true, and honoring to him. James says the tongue is *"a world of unrighteousness,"* among other things:

> And the tongue is a fire, a world of unrighteousness. The tongue is set among our members, staining the whole body, setting on fire the entire course of life, and set on fire by hell. For every kind of beast and bird, of reptile and sea creature, can be tamed and has been tamed by mankind, but no human being can tame the tongue. It is a restless evil, full of deadly poison. With it we bless our Lord and Father, and with it we curse people who are made in the likeness of God. (James 3:6–9)

When I sense that my heart has become numb to the effects of my sinfulness, all I need to do is listen to my mouth or think of the things I should have said but didn't. If I go back over the last few days' blog posts, conversations, and status updates, then my mixed motives and self-glorification become appallingly apparent to me.

It is clear to me that I have no other place to hide except in the righteousness of Christ alone. Nahum 1:6–7 says, "Who can stand before his indignation? Who can endure the heat of his anger? His wrath is poured out like fire, and the rocks are broken into pieces by him. The Lord is good, a stronghold in the day of trouble; he knows those who take refuge in him."

The Love of the Holy Trinity

I want to scratch the surface on that passage from Nahum. When Nahum is proclaiming God's character, he isn't flip-flopping, but we often speak as though we are flip-flopping on the nature of God.

Sometimes when we describe God's character, we unintentionally pit one character trait against another by saying things like, "God is holy, *but* he is loving, too." Nahum describes who God is:

seamlessly holy and loving. God is rightly furious over sin, and God is personal and good.

The Bible doesn't describe God as a schizophrenic in continual conflict in his personality or in the triune godhead. The relationships among the persons of the godhead flow from the perfect character of God—there is no conflict or dilemma in God. God is *unified* in himself to ensure both that he is glorified and that we are secure in his salvation.

For example, God both wrathfully opposes the restless evil of our tongues *and* mercifully delivers us from that sin. God did not create us so that we might debase his character or his creation with slanderous words. The holy Son of God is the lamb who died to redeem men from every nation, tribe, people, and language so they might testify that salvation belongs to God. The Holy Spirit fills us so that we might speak the Word of God with boldness and declare, "Jesus is Lord."

Because God is love, he longs to hear his children sing his praises and rejoice in him. The Father loves the Son as he rejoices to hear his name praised among all the nations. The Spirit loves the Father and the Son, who sent him to bear witness and proclaim the righteousness of God in all the earth.

The wicked, self-serving words that our lips utter come from the overflow of our hearts, and they defile us from the inside out. But God doesn't leave us just as we are in this condition when we repent and believe in Christ. The perfect love and holiness of our triune God assures us that God himself will faithfully forgive us our sins as the blood of Jesus cleanses us from all unrighteousness.

Is Cleanliness Next to Godliness?

I live in an area of the world that is populated with people concerned about spiritual cleanliness. This is wonderful—as it gives me many opportunities to talk with my friends about what defiles a person, how one becomes clean, and how one can remain clean—spiritually-speaking, that is.

My neighbors participate in ceremonial washing to prepare themselves for prayer. One friend told me a story about how she and her husband had a bitter argument while they were doing these washings. I asked her how the angry words exchanged impacted her subsequent offering of prayer. She did not see the connection between her unholy behavior and her unholy-ness.

One friend cleans her bathroom six days a week with an alcohol-based cleaning solution. Germs don't stand a chance in her house! Another friend just takes the bidet hose and sprays water on every surface area in the bathroom and lets it air dry. Both are satisfied with the relative cleanliness.

When I was a kid, I used to think "Cleanliness is next to godliness" was a verse from the Bible. I heard it often and never bothered to consult the Scriptures to see if it was in there. It just made sense to me. But physical cleanliness, in the spiritual terms that Jesus uses, is not next to godliness. Spiritual cleanliness *is* godliness. Spiritual cleanliness is not just the appearance of holiness on the outside. True godliness comes from the inside.

Watch how Jesus uses an ordinary thing like ceremonial hand washing to point to the reality of God's holiness, our sinful nature, and our need for salvation. When the Pharisees questioned Jesus about how his disciples didn't wash their hands according to the religious leaders' traditions, Jesus answered them with a question: "And why do you break the commandment of God for the sake of your tradition?" (Matt. 15:3)

Jesus named a tradition the leaders invented to get around having to obey one of God's commands. Jesus's disciples were not "clean" or "unclean" based on the way they washed their hands before they ate. Jesus explained that what makes a man clean or unclean is his heart:

> Do you not see that whatever goes into the mouth passes into the stomach and is expelled? But what comes out of the mouth proceeds from the heart, and this defiles a person. For out of the heart come evil thoughts, murder, adultery, sexual immorality,

theft, false witness, slander. These are what defile a person. But to eat with unwashed hands does not defile anyone. (Matt. 15:17–20)

What we need more than clean hands is a clean heart. God is the only one who can purify us: "Purge me with hyssop, and I shall be clean; wash me, and I shall be whiter than snow. . . . Create in me a clean heart, O God, and renew a right spirit within me" (Ps. 51:7, 10).

Shame Turned into Joy

What is unique about the cleansing that can only come from God is the response it produces from us. When we experience shame over our sin, our natural tendency is to hide from others. We shut people out of our lives, we avoid praying or Bible reading, and we cover up the evidence of our sin.

The reason my toddler hides the wrappers from stolen candy in the couch cushions is the same reason you and I might "miss" a phone call or "lose" an e-mail from a friend who is pursuing us. It's the same reason we might make up excuses for neglecting fellowship and not going to church.

I love the honesty of my friend. I didn't get to see her at our church meeting one week, although I knew she was there somewhere. I was looking for her because we had made plans that I would follow up with her about something. I said, "Hey, I missed chatting with you last week!" She said, "Yeah, I know. I was avoiding you. Sorry about that." My friend openly confessed that she was hiding from accountability. Do you see how she didn't give shame an opportunity to fester in her heart? She confessed with clarity and honesty.

We hide because we feel shame, and we're fearful of being shamed by others. That's why Adam and Eve made coverings from fig leaves and hid from God when they sinned in the garden.

Back in Psalm 51, what does King David request after he asks for forgiveness? In exchange for the shame of his sin, David asks the Lord to give him joy: "Let me hear joy and gladness; let the bones that you have broken rejoice" (v. 8); "Restore to me the joy of your salvation, and uphold me with a willing spirit" (v. 12). Shame tells us to hide, but joy spills out in praise to God for his salvation.

Instead of hiding, what does David say he will do? "Then I will teach transgressors your ways, and sinners will return to you" (v. 13). "Deliver me from bloodguiltiness, O God, O God of my salvation, and my tongue will sing aloud of your righteousness" (v. 14). "O Lord, open my lips, and my mouth will declare your praise" (v. 15). Only a tongue that has been loosed by God's grace can sing like that. Only a heart that has been cleansed by God's grace will bare itself to the world as a testimony to God's mercy and righteousness.

What did Adam and Eve encounter when the Lord confronted them? He gave them grace and covered their nakedness with the skin of an animal he had slaughtered on their behalf, and he promised a Savior who would forever take away their shame (Gen. 3:15).

Grace Is Greater Than Our Sin

This kind of grace is worth singing about. Hymn writer Julia Johnston wrote,

> Sin and despair, like the sea waves cold,
> Threaten the soul with infinite loss;
> Grace that is greater, yes, grace untold,
> Points to the refuge, the mighty cross.
>
> Dark is the stain that we cannot hide.
> What can avail to wash it away?
> Look! There is flowing a crimson tide,
> Brighter than snow you may be today.[1]

William Cowper, though plagued with madness and acute depression, knew with clarity of heart and soul that his sin was dealt with on the cross when he wrote:

> There is a fountain filled with blood drawn from
>   Emmanuel's veins;
> And sinners plunged beneath that flood lose all their
>   guilty stains.

> Lose all their guilty stains, lose all their guilty stains;
> And sinners plunged beneath that flood lose all their
>   guilty stains.[2]

Robert Lowry penned these famous lines in his hymn "Nothing but the Blood":

> What can wash away my sin?
> Nothing but the blood of Jesus;
> What can make me whole again?
> Nothing but the blood of Jesus.[3]

The greatest nightmare of shame is the fear of being found out. But the gospel turns this fear into an occasion for joyful celebration at the foot of the cross. We will be free from the controlling effect of shame only when we are repenting of our efforts to cleanse ourselves and rejoicing in the saving blood of Christ instead.

"When Will _____ Ever Change?!"

You may be thinking, *This all sounds well and good. But . . .* Perhaps the "but" is personally directed at yourself. You wonder if you'll ever change. Or perhaps your concern is directed toward others. You wonder if they will ever change.

Even though we can recite verses from Scripture about God adopting us into his family and making us joint heirs with his Son, we still despair about our potential growth in godliness. Even though we can discuss our well-developed view of God's goals in redemptive history, we doubt his willingness to save *us*. We find it hard to believe God is willing to save the people in *our* lives.

We're sinners who are saints living in the tension of an already/not yet kingdom. No wonder we're prone to discouragement! If we're honest with ourselves, at times we may even be tempted to think that God himself is fed up with us and all our sin, baggage, and issues. This is one reason we desperately need to be encouraged by one another! Even Paul tells us how he needs encouragement from others: "For I long to see you, that I may impart to you some spiritual gift to strengthen you—that is, that we may be mutually encouraged by each other's faith, both yours and mine" (Rom. 1:11–12).

Once there was a woman so critical that other women sometimes felt intimidated when talking with her. One friend in particular would avoid talking with her in social settings and, in time, neglected to pursue their friendship by keeping in touch. Years went by. After a while, neither woman noticed her loss—not the critical woman or the intimidated woman. Then something began to change. God was growing them both to more resemble the likeness of his Son. By God's grace, the critical woman began to wake up to the fact of her pride and saw how it offended God. Repenting, she started rejoicing in Jesus's superiority and brilliance instead of in her arrogance.

Apparently the change was noticeable to the friend who had been so intimidated earlier on. After four years of emotional distance, she boldly reached out to reestablish their friendship, no longer threatened by the formerly arrogant woman's potential for and likelihood of judging her. God's kindness leads to repentance! That arrogant woman who reeked of pride and biting criticism is me, and the intimidated woman is actually several of my girlfriends. Praise God for his grace! I'm aware that this is an ongoing struggle, but I taste the victory Jesus can give over this sin when I apprehend it by his grace through faith.

Unbelief Is Not Impossible to Overcome

I know that sometimes singing with any amount of confidence "It Is Well with My Soul" is difficult. Struggles with discouragement and doubt shouldn't be kept in the dark. We need to have others in our lives reminding us that Christ is our champion who has defeated sin, death, and Satan. Submit yourself to your local church and commit to serving alongside its members. Find another believer in your local church with whom you can pray and discuss what you're learning in God's Word. Discuss the sermons and pray together through your church's membership directory. Make an effort to be intentionally involved in each other's lives outside of casual greetings at the weekly worship gathering and the occasional small chats interspersed throughout your week. Make that phone call to set a time to meet or send that e-mail or SMS to start connecting with someone today. Come ready to ask good questions, be a good listener, and bring your Bible so you can look into God's Word together.

These suggestions aren't a magic recipe to cure discouragement, but God has prescribed fellowship with other believers as one of the means he uses to release gospel truth into our lives.

We all need to be reminded of God's commitment to finish the good work he has started. Paul assures us that God is not a procrastinator: "And I am sure of this, that he who began a good work in you will bring it to completion at the day of Jesus Christ. It is right for me to feel this way about you all, because I hold you in my heart, for you are all partakers with me of grace, both in my imprisonment and in the defense and confirmation of the gospel" (Phil. 1:6–7).

By God's grace, he is triumphant even over your hopelessness, cynicism, and doubt. This is true for you even if you've labeled yourself as hopeless. This is true for you even if you've been avoiding accountability like the plague. This is true for you even if you've flipped every confrontation into an opportunity to "bite the hand that feeds you." This is true for you even if years have gone by and you feel that nothing has changed.

God in his grace invites us to be continually repenting of our sins and rejoicing in Christ's provision of righteousness for us. Because we are so prone to discouragement over our sanctification, we must saturate ourselves in Scripture to remind ourselves of the truth. I know, for my own part, my skepticism of my potential for growth or someone else's is rooted in a faulty view of who God is and the implications of his gospel. I realize that last statement requires quite a bit of unpacking—entire books have been written about this. For the sake of brevity I'll share a few things that I've asked others to remind me of on this subject:

When you are cynical that God will never change this or that about you, or you surmise that so-and-so might be a lost cause, your unbelief is rooted in one or both of these lies: (1) God is not *able* to free sinners from their sin; and (2) God is not *willing* to free sinners from their sin.

But God is able. The power that raised Christ Jesus from the dead is the same power that works in the hearts of those who believe (Eph. 1:19–20).

And God is willing. The desire that compelled the Father to willingly give his Son for us all is the same desire that motivates him to finish what he's begun (Rom. 8:28–32).

Furthermore God's commitment to save those who believe on him is to the praise of his glory. Consider the great lengths to which the Lord has gone to secure you in him. "In him you also, when you heard the word of truth, the gospel of your salvation, and believed in him, were sealed with the promised Holy Spirit, who is the guarantee of our inheritance until we acquire possession of it, to the praise of his glory" (Eph. 1:13–14). The holy Trinity is working on your behalf for your salvation and for the glory of God!

Struggle Together to Believe the Gospel

Believing that these things are true about God and about ourselves is not easy. Confidence in Christ is a work of faith, and there are many faith squelchers in the world. Our faith is under attack from the lies of the Devil, the spiritually dulling influence of the world, and even the hardness of our own hearts.

When we struggle to believe that the gospel is true, our hearts need reassurance. Reminding ourselves of gospel truth will "reassure our heart before him; for whenever our heart condemns us, God is greater than our heart" (1 John 3:19–20). But our hearts may not always relinquish the burden of shame so willingly. John Ensor says that especially in those times "we must grasp the truth of the cross and wrestle our conscience into alignment and conformity. We must instruct our conscience about the cross until our conviction of guilt gives way to joy and confidence. Hebrews 10:22 calls this having 'our hearts sprinkled clean from an evil [burdened] conscience.'"4

Our hearts cannot be the end-all authorities on truth. Only God can claim that right. Sometimes we really do need to wrestle our hearts into submission to God's truth—Martin Luther–style. When your heart throws your sins in your face, say, "I admit that I deserve death and hell. So what! Because I know the one who suffered and made satisfaction on my behalf. His name is Jesus Christ, Son of God, and where he is, there I shall be also."

God will not hold sins against you that he has held onto his Son's dying body on the cross. Those sins are paid in full. This is the truth that sets you free! And if the Son sets you free, you will be free indeed (John 8:32–36).

Our heavenly Father will never ever write off any of his children. The Holy Spirit guarantees this by his indwelling presence. Jesus, the bridegroom of the church, is about his work of purifying his bride:

> Husbands, love your wives, as Christ loved the church and gave himself up for her, that he might sanctify her, having cleansed her by the washing of water with the word, so that he might present the church to himself in splendor, without spot or wrinkle or any such thing, that she might be holy and without blemish. (Eph. 5:25–27)

Let that truth sink into every nook and cranny of your heart. Wash yourself in the word of the gospel. Repeat. (No rinsing necessary.)

9

God's Abiding Presence in Our Pain

I don't want to get much further into this book before I share with you more of where I'm coming from.

Obviously, It Isn't Obvious to Everyone

You've probably already gathered that I'm a wife and mother with three young children. My husband is a pastor and we live in the Middle East. We live in the upstairs portion of a villa that also houses the church offices and serves as meeting space for weekly Bible studies and the like. I like to cook in mass quantities for two main reasons—the containers look so neat and tidy in my freezer, and I have a wild streak of sheer laziness in me. Just thaw dinner the night before and pop it in the oven half an hour before you need to eat? Yes, please!

But something that is not readily apparent about me is the same thing that you don't notice about most people, although it is true of everyone you meet. Proverbs 14:13 says that even in laughter the heart may ache.

I live in the midst of pain.

We're *all* carrying some sort of burden—maybe it's a lost love or a lost child, a broken friendship or a broken home. We all limp as we go about our daily lives, and sometimes the pain is so deep that we can hardly bear to stand up.

When I introduced my working definition of the mundane

as the normalcy of your daily life, I'm certain that some of you cringed as you read it. Your mundane isn't simple or ordinary, by any means. Your daily life is marked by complicated situations and extraordinary pain. I can only imagine what pain is represented in those who read these words.

Yesterday morning a Christian teacher was mercilessly shot to death because he was telling his neighbors about Jesus. The murderers plotted against him, stalked him, and filled his body with bullets. I woke up this morning praying for his family; my heart is very heavy for his wife and their children. Most of us don't live in the daily reality of being killed for our faith, which Jesus said is a strong potential (Luke 11:49). But the daily mundane for this small family is marked by martyrdom.

One year ago this week some precious friends of ours lost their two-year-old son in a car accident. Not a mundane moment goes by when they aren't aware of their loss. They would also say that not a moment goes by when the Lord is not aware of their pain, too. His abiding presence is a grace to their grieving hearts.

Both of these families hope in Christ and his triumph over their pain. My story is different from theirs, and so is yours. But the same God who ministers to them in the pain of their mundane can give us grace, too.

I hope my story of God's faithfulness encourages you. In sharing my story I want to point you to the one who daily bears us up (Ps. 68:19) and has borne our griefs and carried our sorrows in his own body (Isa. 53:4).

Broken Arms and Broken Hearts

When you hear me say that we shouldn't bank our hope on our earthly circumstances and that we should put our trust in Christ alone, it comes from a heart that's been broken over trusting in things that don't deliver.

When I was pregnant with our first child, my husband lost major function in both of his arms because of a genetic nerve disease. He was typing in a seminary class when his fingers started tingling. The tingling soon developed into pain. He began to lose fine motor skills such as buttoning his shirt, shaving his beard, typing papers, turning keys, and writing with pens. Muscle atrophy also took effect, and things like books, doors, babies, and metal utensils became too heavy for him to lift.

We were distraught as my husband was in constant pain. By the time the baby was born, my husband's pain had moved all the way up to his elbow. Before our daughter's first birthday, his other arm was afflicted as well. In the meantime, we were seeking just about every physical solution available to us at the time.

Personally, I was optimistic. I took every positive comment that people and medical professionals made as a guarantee from God, even though they made no such guarantees. I think I was largely hopeful that modern medicine had a solution for us, because I wanted to be distracted from the looming reality that these circumstances could get worse. Plus being hopeful felt a lot better than being depressed.

But it wasn't long before depression fell on our family like a landslide. My husband had just had a successful surgery on both of his elbows to release the entrapped nerves, and he was recovering quite well. We were ecstatic that finally he might begin to improve physically and be healed once and for all. That summer we were ready to move abroad and begin the work of church planting, so we sold all of our stuff (except our books), packed a few suitcases of clothes, and made all the arrangements to move to the balmy desert of the Arabian Peninsula.

When we landed, everything was going as expected with physical therapy, culture adjustments, and all the other challenges we knew we would have to face once we got here. What we weren't expecting was for my husband's physical condition to further deteriorate. For some reason we do not know, within the span of one week after some intense driving in a crowded parking lot, the burning, stabbing pain was back in his arms. The pain wasn't gradually increasing like before—this time it was back with a vengeance.

God, Where Are You?

I cannot begin to describe to you how alarming this experience was. Our oldest daughter was now eighteen months old, and she began to have nightmares that would send her hurtling off of her mattress, which was on the floor. I held her while she tossed and turned and struggled to sleep. I was pregnant with our second daughter and began to experience extreme fatigue that lasted for the duration of the second and third trimesters. All of this was in the midst of culture-crossing stress and trying to learn to function in the midst of a new language. When we woke up in the mornings we would pray for the day to pass by quickly, and when the nights came I would watch my insomniac husband pace the floor in agonizing pain while I lay in bed sick to my stomach, praying that the morning would come soon.

In moments of spiritual clarity in the middle of that desert I would sing this line from a cherished hymn over and over in my mind:

> My hope is built on nothing less
> than Jesus' blood and righteousness.
> I dare not trust the sweetest frame,
> but wholly lean on Jesus' name.
> On Christ the solid Rock I stand,
> all other ground is sinking sand;
> all other ground is sinking sand.

It was the hope of the gospel, and the gospel alone, that kept us during that time. It is the hope of the gospel that keeps us even today. Our physical circumstances are somewhat relieved, as we've now lived in this country for several years and have learned how to function quite well. But my husband is still in pain. This testimony of God's faithfulness doesn't have a neatly tied bow on it with "and we all lived happily ever after and God answered my prayers just the way I thought he would."

More than five years later, I am still the sole physical caregiver for our now three children. At times over these past five years, I have also been the sole physical caregiver for my husband. Sometimes when his nerve pain flares up, or when he's recovering from a surgery, I need to help him bathe and get dressed, open doors for him, feed him, drive him to and from meetings, brush and floss his teeth, pick up his books, take notes or type, and pull back the sheets of the bed so he can get in. On one occasion I walked into the bathroom to find him splayed out on the floor with a knot on the back of his head. He had stumbled getting out of the shower and hit his head because he doesn't have the arm strength to catch himself. He's fallen down stairs before. Those of us who have healthy arms take for granted how much we use them to maintain our balance.

I can see the grace of God at work in my life in the midst of this. For several years I felt a choking fear that Dave would die in an accident that could have been preventable if his arms were strong. This is still a possibility, but over time the grace of God is teaching me not to live in fear of the unknown. Dying to self and serving my husband has also been difficult, but by God's grace, now when Dave asks me to help him with something, my first reaction isn't usually to involuntarily clench my jaw to try and choke back bitter tears at the lot God has given us. And I know that his grace is sufficient for me when I do struggle to serve.

During these seasons that are particularly difficult for us, our mundane is punctuated by a crying baby or a whining toddler. That's when I have to sing that line from my favorite hymn out loud!

God Is Good, All the Time

We say, "God is good," when our children are obedient, we don't feel any pain, the house is in order, and we spent two cheerful hours doing homemade crafts together without any whining. And we would be right to say so. But God is good for deeper reasons than our experience of temporary relief in fluctuating earthly circumstances.

How quickly our perspective changes when we're thrown the proverbial curveball. I've been discouraged over the things I deal with because of my husband's chronic pain. I've been devastated to hear my child's teacher remark on how my daughter has behaved disrespectfully. I was so upset that I gave myself a week-long splitting headache when the central air-conditioning broke in August. A friend of mine developed gastric reflux during a year-long dispute with her neighbor over fixing the fence that divided their properties. Another friend lost 15 pounds from worry and stress in the month her husband lost his job.

I've never prayed so hard for Christ to "just come back quickly" as the time when my baby bit me and then went on a nursing strike, and I was almost admitted to the hospital for mastitis and a staph infection from the wound. Those are the mundane moments that make you want to curl up into a ball in the corner. And on more than a few occasions I did just that. On a few excruciatingly difficult days my husband has found me sitting on the floor in our walk-in closet bawling my eyes out.

Those are extreme moments. There are also less extreme moments, like those in the mostly uneventful days when something just feels off between my husband and me. We pass each other in the hallway and just feel disconnected and weird. Sometimes days will go by when I haven't sat down for a meal because I'm so busy feeding three hungry little ones and possibly some guests. I suddenly realize—wow, the only time I have sat down in the past four days is to go to sleep at night. There are also days when sin gets the best of me, and I spend the entire day complaining that I must have woken up on the wrong side of the bed. By 10:00 a.m. I am ready to call it a day and send the kids to bed because I'm so cranky. How good does God feel in those mundane moments?

There's a saying I learned in Kenya when visiting the church there. When somebody says, "God is good," everybody answers, "All the time." We extol the character of God and affirm, "God doesn't change." But how does God's immutable character affect our everyday perspective on life? If God doesn't change, how are we to respond when our circumstances do change? Rejoicing in the unchanging character of God is much harder to do when you feel like your life is a sandstorm swirling all around you, and you can't see which way to go, much less where the road went.

Gutsy Prayer Requests

Martin Luther said, "Although it hurts us when he takes his own from us, his good will should be a greater comfort to us than all his gifts, for God is immeasurably better than all his gifts."[1] That is a very gutsy thing to say. That's gutsy because one must be certain of two things. First, one must have faith that no hurt can be so painful that God is not able to comfort the hurting one. Second, one must have faith that no gift from God could ever be greater than the gift of himself. That's a gutsy thing to say and an even gutsier thing to try and live. And the gutsiest thing to do is to pray on a daily basis that God would show you how this is true.

Are your palms sweating yet? Mine are. Because we ask God to do this all the time. Did you realize that?

This is what we're asking for when we ask God to show us mercy or give us grace. This is what we're asking for when we pray for relief from our painful circumstances. This is what we're asking for when we ask for future grace for some challenge that is just around the corner. Whenever we say to the Lord as Moses did, "Please show me your glory" (Ex. 33:18), we are asking God to make us glad in him. The only way that God answers prayer is in accordance with his perfect character. God cannot do anything that is *not* to the praise of his glory.

When God answers our prayers, he will always answer according to his will for our lives, that is, in accordance with his will for us to be sanctified (1 Thess. 4:3).

Every time God acts, he acts in righteousness and grace. The God who is immeasurably better than all his gifts and is the standard of perfect righteousness could never answer a prayer request for grace by giving you a gift less than himself. He's a good Father who doesn't give his children rocks and snakes, but bread to sustain their lives and make them glad.

God Doesn't Give His Children Pacifiers

God is also not accustomed to giving his children pacifiers to keep them quiet so they'll forget they need him and then leave him alone.

Sadly, sometimes when we pray we think God ought to give us the pacifier we've requested. We know that the thing we're asking for is less than God, but we still want it because it will make us temporarily happy.

The pacifier that I scrounge around for is usually peace and quiet. When I say "peace and quiet," I usually mean that I want my children to sleep in late so that I can have "me-[centered] time." I even pray for my kids to sleep later so that I can delay the time when I have to serve their needs. The first peep I hear from one of them is usually met with an inward groan from me: "It's too early to start today! All I want is some peace and quiet."

I too easily forget that God is the one who quiets my soul. When my soul is quieted within me, it doesn't matter how much noise is going on around me. I too easily forget that God is my peace. When God is my peace, then rockets could be going off around my house, my husband's health could drastically decline, and I could lack a single moment alone, and still be at peace.

Oh, how many times have I asked for pacifiers! These pacifier prayers usually start with this: "Lord, if you would just _____ for me, then everything would be okay." I have an idea of what it is that I want or need, and I ask God to fill my order—in my name. Prayers like this typically involve comfort and never involve requests regarding my sanctification or God's glory. Bryan Chappell, in his excellent book *Praying Backwards* (which is my favorite book on prayer), says that we ought always pray in Jesus's name, that is, with his intentions to glorify the Father in mind.[2] Oh how my prayer life would change if I began my prayers by asking, "In Jesus's name, Father, would you _____?"

Praise God that Jesus is the final prophet who frees us from the delusion of our own wisdom. He's our Great High Priest who sacrificed himself as the atonement for our sins. Jesus is our king who liberates captives from the chains of sin and self-governance. God in his grace does not always rescue us from difficult or painful circumstances. God is about his business of redeeming us while we are in the midst of this broken world. He is delivering us from something far more dangerous and grievous to our souls—he's saving us from our sin.

For God to give his children whom he loves an insufficient, temporary fix would be contrary to his desire to satisfy our souls for all eternity.

> You make known to me the path of life;
>   in your presence there is fullness of joy;
>   at your right hand are pleasures forevermore. (Ps. 16:11)

> Come, everyone who thirsts,
>   come to the waters;
> and he who has no money,
>   come, buy and eat!
> Come, buy wine and milk
>   without money and without price.
> Why do you spend your money for that which is not bread,
>   and your labor for that which does not satisfy?
> Listen diligently to me, and eat what is good,
>   and delight yourselves in rich food.
> Incline your ear, and come to me;
>   hear, that your soul may live;
> and I will make with you an everlasting covenant,
>   my steadfast, sure love for David. (Isa. 55:1–3)

> I will greatly rejoice in the Lord;
>   my soul shall exult in my God,

for he has clothed me with the garments of salvation;
    he has covered me with the robe of righteousness,
as a bridegroom decks himself like a priest with a
      beautiful headdress,
    and as a bride adorns herself with her jewels. (Isa. 61:10)

For I will satisfy the weary soul, and every languishing soul I will replenish. (Jer. 31:25)

My flesh and my heart may fail,
    but God is the strength of my heart and my portion forever.
    (Ps. 73:26).

One Man's Silver Pacifiers

When we grieve over our difficult circumstances here on earth, the gospel comforts us by reminding us that Jesus has gone before us to prepare a place for us in his Father's house. When we're tempted to revel in our favorable circumstances, or modern medicine, or people who make promises they can't keep, or money that promises us security, the gospel humbles us through the reminder that the steadfast love of the Lord is *better than life.*

There's a story in the book of Judges about a man who believed in God but loved his pacifiers more than he loved God. Micah wasn't content to worship God alone, so he made some silver idols to keep around his house. No harm in keeping a few pacifiers around to make yourself happy, right? Micah quickly realized that he still felt distant from God. It's like he had an itch to scratch, but the idols he made just couldn't reach it. Micah thought that what he needed to close the gap between himself and God was his very own priest. Paying for a personal priest was clearly not in line with the way God had prescribed for his children to worship him. Nonetheless, Micah managed to recruit a Levite to be his family's personal priest. Micah said, "Now I know that the LORD will prosper me, because I have a Levite as a priest" (Judg. 17:13).

Micah was happy with the idols he made and the priest he hired. Trouble soon fell upon Micah's household when some

Danites were passing through the area and heard about Micah's pacifiers. The Danites wanted these things for themselves, so they ransacked Micah's house, stole the silver idols, and convinced the priest to come be their priest instead.

Of course, Micah was devastated when he discovered what had happened. He mustered some friends and neighbors together and pursued the Danites. When Micah and company confronted the Danites they made such a scene that the thieves said, "What is the matter with you, that you come with such a company?" (Judg. 18:23).

Micah's answer reveals the dismal state of his soul: "You take my gods that I made and the priest, and go away, and what have I left? How then do you ask me, 'What is the matter with you?'" (v. 24).

What have I left? Have you ever said that before? I know I have.

We're not too different from Micah. When our circumstances are difficult and our mundane is painful, and when we do not value the peace we have with God, we sound like Micah. "What do you mean, 'What is the matter with me?'" we protest. "You've taken everything I need to be happy and left me with nothing. *Nothing!*"

When God mercifully strips us of our idols, he has in mind to give us something better instead—himself.

In the midst of a painful mundane, by God's grace we can echo the psalmist, "I say to the LORD, 'You are my Lord; I have no good apart from you'" (Ps. 16:2). The cry of our heart changes from "What have I left?" to "Whom have I in heaven but you? And there is nothing on earth that I desire besides you. My flesh and my heart may fail, but God is the strength of my heart and my portion forever" (Ps. 73:25–26).

I know it may seem so precarious to stake your joy not on your circumstances, or even on the gifts that God has given you, but on the person of God himself. I know that's difficult. That's why we need faith to do it. We need faith to trust that God doesn't merely "know what's best for us," but that he *is* what's best for us no matter what our circumstances are.

"Jesus answered them, 'This is the work of God, that you believe in him whom he has sent'" (John 6:29). When we believe in Jesus to provide all that we need for life and godliness, we can confess with tears of joyful relief, "For from him and through him and to him are all things. To him be glory forever. Amen" (Rom. 11:36).

10

United with Christ but Lonely for Friends

As I'm writing this chapter, my girls are going through an intense phase in which they can hardly do anything without annoying each other. There isn't a single toy or piece of clothing in their room over which they can't conjure up an argument.

Sometimes their arguments make me want to just throw all of their toys into a trash bag and leave it on the side of the road for some mythical children who won't fight over the toys. But the toys and the clothes aren't the problem.

The Annoyance Olympics extends into the car as well. "Why do I have to sit in the back?" "She's kicking my seat." "Unbuckle me first, not her." "No, it's my turn to climb out Daddy's side." But the car isn't the problem, either.

The games continue into the public arena. This is where the intensity of their "annoyification" really ramps up. Dozens of innocent bystanders can get sucked into their fantastical world of preschool-style power plays when they argue in public.

Sometimes I imagine myself with an amp and a microphone to inform passersby, "Hi! Welcome to our demonstration of human depravity. What are they fighting about, you ask? Well, let me tell you. The featured argument from 9:00 a.m. to 9:06 a.m. is a petty disagreement over lip balm. Whose lip balm is more sparkly? And whose is pink and whose is purple? Step right up, folks, and witness our family's validation of the doctrine of original sin. Stick around a few more minutes to watch a brawl over whose turn it is for anything—you name it!"

When Is It My Turn?

My prevailing feeling is one of discouragement, sometimes embarrassment, and most often loneliness. "I'm the only person in the whole world who feels beaten down," I tell myself. Silly, isn't it? It's a discipline to remind myself that I'm not alone. Sometimes I call or e-mail my mother to commiserate over our shared experiences with moderating sibling squabbles like this. Mom raised three young ladies with the same age differences as my children. Last week I wrote this to my mom in an e-mail:

> Mom, the girls are fighting over a single doll when there are a dozen dolls strewn about their feet. I am SO sorry for all the grief we caused you when we were little stinkers (and big stinkers)! Wow! You have the patience and forbearance of a . . . of a, well, I don't know who or what is more patient than God. So thank you for being patient like God. I love you so much!

Mom tells me to hang in there. Sometimes she encourages me with candor like this: "This is exactly how you and your sisters were for years!" *Years.* My girls are only three and nearly five years old right now. I need God's grace and something baked with peanut butter and chocolate.

Do feelings of loneliness threaten to overwhelm you, too? No wonder it's easy to feel isolated when you're wading waist deep in waters like these. When you're keeping a home—with kids or not—there's never a dull moment, but the loneliness can still settle onto your heart like dust settles after a thorough sweeping.

The question "When is it my turn?" is one we ask our whole lives. The subject changes as we age, but the question remains the same. We want know when it's our turn to get what we want. "What about me?" is the primary question we ask in our battle for contentment.

When your life is all things routine, sometimes you feel as if it's never going to be your turn to have a meaningful social life. I totally understand that. Every week I have to pass up social opportunities because of my life's circumstances. I am so prone to feeling discouraged by this. If I'm not vigilant in keeping my attitude in check, discouragement gives way to entitlement that breeds bitterness in my heart.

We homemakers need to have a gospel-centered perspective on our relationships, especially if we're prone to loneliness and the discontentment that sometimes flows from feeling isolated.

Free to Be the Friend We Want

When I was in high school the American television show *Friends* launched their pilot episode. Six friends doing life together—it seemed so perfect. I remember thinking that I couldn't wait to be a real grown-up and have awesome friends just like that. Even their conflicts were idealized!

So many of us homemakers lament over our friendships. We are real people living real lives, and we want real friends. While we may have acquaintances we talk to throughout our day, at church, and as we go about our business around town, these relationships might be mostly shallow and circumstantial. We still feel lonely even though we have friends and stay connected to them through social media.

We sincerely desire to invest in friendships in which we can practice the "one anothers" from Scripture, such as bear with one another in love (Eph. 4:2) and comfort one another (2 Cor. 13:11). But how can we "bear one another's burdens, and so fulfill the law of Christ" (Gal. 6:2) if we don't have close friendships?

Of first importance in having good friends is being a good friend to others. So what are the obstacles to being a good friend?

Many factors hinder our ability to be a good friend. The first reason that comes to mind is that we are naturally self-centered. We suffer from delusional preoccupations over things like sparkly lip balm and whose turn it is to be married, have children, buy a house, bedazzle said house, and have the wonderful life we've always dreamed of. Our sin is an obstacle to friendships. Selfishness, pride, apathy, and envy are walls that separate us from significant friendships.

Beyond the sin nature that we all share may be the genuine lack of time that is necessary for friendships. We may have misplaced priorities and other complicating life circumstances. I don't know about you, but I could write my own name next to all of those reasons and excuses and own them. The first person I think about in the morning is me. I go about my day focused on preserving the dignity of me. I prioritize my day and night according to what I think I need. And I go to bed at night wondering how to make tomorrow all about me.

When you add the entitlement of "it's my turn" into the mix, it's like a multiplying yeast, and the ingredients swell together into a loaf of bitterness. The more excuses I make for my lack of effort to work on friendships, the more entitled I feel. The batter overflows from the pan and drips onto the heating element at the bottom of the oven, burning and filling my kitchen with smoke. That's how our sin nature works.

But the gospel of Jesus Christ says that even despite our sin and our issues, we can have freedom to be real friends to others. Consider Galatians 5:13-15:

> For you were called to freedom, brothers. Only do not use your freedom as an opportunity for the flesh, but through love serve one another. For the whole law is fulfilled in one word: "You shall love your neighbor as yourself." But if you bite and devour one another, watch out that you are not consumed by one another.

That is an admonition to live in the freedom of the gospel, an instruction to use that freedom for good and not evil, and a warning of the consequences for choosing poorly.

Having freedom in Christ means that we can be free from the sin that comes between friends. Friends who have been estranged can instead be united in Christ. Friends who are distant can be brought near to one another as they are brought near to God by the blood of Christ. Friends who are different can find commonality in their faith in the life, death, and resurrection of Jesus.

Your Turn to Let Grace Change You

I've struggled with the same ongoing issue in my friendships since I was two years old. "She hit me first" is my go-to excuse for not pursuing relationships with other women. For example, if a friend offends me—whether she meant to or not—I am less willing to open myself up to her in the future. What I am open to instead is manipulating future interactions with her so that I feel like I am in control of the friendship. I intentionally avoid talking about myself and letting this friend know me; it's even couched in my asking intentional questions to cover up my lack of sharing. This is not the way of love that the Bible talks about.

The security we have in Christ that is initiated by grace, enacted by grace, and preserved by grace changes the way we relate to one another *first by changing us*. As the fruit of the Holy Spirit grows in our lives, we no longer reap a harvest of relationships marked by self-interest, manipulation, and power plays.

The liberating power of the gospel allows us to reach into each other's lives and ask good, soul-searching questions. And not as a cover-up for our lack of self-disclosure! We can ask these questions because we're free to think of others before we think of ourselves. We don't have to be afraid of the answers we hear, because we trust in the God who raises the dead and always finishes the good work he's started.

We can confess our sins to one another because in Christ we are forgiven and are able to forgive others. We can bear one another's burdens and help relieve each other's difficult circumstances because we're concerned for our neighbors' souls.

We can keep each other's "crazy" in check because we're hopeful in God's future grace that Christ is coming back and he wants us to hold onto our hope in him until the end. We can lock arms together and be *for* one another instead of competing against each other, because we're all looking to the reward. He shows us grace and kindness "so that in the coming ages he might show the immeasurable riches of his grace in kindness toward us in Christ Jesus" (Eph. 2:7).

I've had tastes of God's victorious grace over my sin of selfishness. How I long to be free of the bonds of self-centered manipulation and entitlement! What a feast of grace it would be if we all believed it was "our turn" to let God's grace change us.

If Christ dwells in our hearts through faith, then we can be rooted and grounded in his love. By his grace we can have the strength we need to comprehend the magnitude of his love for us that surpasses knowledge so that we are filled with all the fullness of God (Eph. 3:17–19). Because Jesus loved us first, it's always our turn to bask in his love and go and love others.

What If?

Many of the excuses and reasons for not investing in deep friendships come with a "what if" fear. These "what ifs" can be debilitating.

As a pastor's wife, mother to young children, and member of an expatriate church, I can certainly understand how circumstances can make friendships difficult to maintain. The reluctance to begin taking steps toward building into relationships can be motivated by feelings of futility. How can I possibly find time to invest in friends when I am so busy at home? What if I do all of these things to make friendships work and my effort isn't reciprocated or appreciated? What if I invest so much of myself in someone, only for her to move away to another country in a year? Can I responsibly initiate new friendships when I might not have time? What if it's awkward to try to have a conversation about something that is beyond the typical "What did you put in this soup?" and "Did you hear such-and-such store is having a sale?"

What if you bend over backwards to rearrange your schedule

to spend time with a friend and she doesn't have the courtesy to call when she's not able to meet with you? What if you prioritize relationships to the neglect of your household duties, but others won't do the same for you? What if you go above and beyond to live out the "one another" commands in Scripture in your community, yet it feels as if nobody is taking care of you?

The bigger question we ought to be asking ourselves is not all of these "what ifs." What we need to ask ourselves is this: Am I willing to welcome others into my life just as Jesus welcomed me into his?

If these "what if" questions have ever driven your decision making in regard to relationships, the blessing in Romans 15:5–7 is both strengthening and instructive: "May the God of endurance and encouragement grant you to live in such harmony with one another, in accord with Christ Jesus, that together you may with one voice glorify the God and Father of our Lord Jesus Christ. Therefore welcome one another as Christ has welcomed you, for the glory of God."

The way that Christ has welcomed us is through his sacrificial life and death in service to people who did not and could not reciprocate his generosity. Now, by the energy of Christ that so powerfully works in us (Col. 1:29), we can welcome others.

Turning Wall Builders into Bridge Builders

What does it look like *practically* to welcome others like Jesus did?

I am tempted to give you a list of practical suggestions, such as how to order your schedule or initiate discipleship relationships in which homemakers just "do life together." I love practical steps because they make nice to-do lists, and I can write them on my kitchen whiteboard, set reminders in my mobile phone, and check them off the list when I've done them. The appendix of this book could even include a reproducible template of a checklist of ten steps to be a good friend, so you can be guaranteed that your efforts will be fruitful.

Of course, there are practical adjustments you ought to make to your daily routine to allow time for friendships. For example, if you hang signs outside your gate that say, "No Friends Allowed" or "Beware: Lonely Homemaker Brooding," you might have a hard time finding people who are willing to give friendship with you a chance.

Practically speaking, there are walls that need to be torn down or at least have doors carved into them through lifestyle tweaks and adjustments. But just knocking a hole in the wall doesn't tear down the wall or prevent another one from being built in its place.

Don't misunderstand: renovating the walls in our lives is not wrong; it's just insufficient because it doesn't address our heart issue at its foundation. I like how biblical counselor Deepak Reju said, "Addressing the circumstances without addressing the heart is like offering a drink of water to a man who is on fire. It's not wrong, it's just insufficient."[1]

If a homemaker has built walls around herself that obstruct genuine friendships, she must punch a few holes in the walls to make windows for others to see inside and for her to see out. Then she must be willing to drop the boards, nails, and hammers that she uses to build more walls. Then she must build bridges instead.

But why would a wall builder want to build bridges? To borrow a phrase from Scottish theologian and mathematician Thomas Chalmers, only the "expulsive power of a new affection" can turn a wall builder into a bridge builder. The new affection that displaces our desire to remain self-oriented is the glory of God as seen in the gospel.

Love, the Fruit of Confession, the Fruit of Worship

I'll use my most potent friend-repellant sin as an example. Let's say that I try psychologizing myself into being less prideful and more friendly. First, I want to identify what it is about me that keeps me from making friends. Through thoughtful introspection I realize that I'm prideful. I declare, "Hi, my name is God. Er... sorry. See, this is part of the problem. I'm not God; my name is Gloria. I'm a prideful person. I think I'm pretty great and think others ought to think I'm pretty great, too." There, I admitted it. My verbal confession just fixed my pride problem, right?

Wrong. Until change has taken place in my heart, just saying that I'm prideful bears no lasting fruit in my life. Distinctly Christian confession deals with sin in that it involves genuine repentance. We feel regret primarily over how it separates us from God, who ought to be our joy.

Being able to name our idolatrous affections, identify our sins, and own responsibility for them is critical to our repentance and faithful obedience to the gospel. If you're not sure what your idolatrous affections might be, or you're at a loss for how you've been sinful, just ask your spouse or your friends. They might hesitate at first to tell you, but it's not because they're doubtful that you're a sinner. They're trying to figure out how to break the news to you.

I'm so thankful that I have friends who will shoot me straight in this area. They're more concerned with God being honored in my life than with me feeling happy with them. Sure, sometimes conversations about our sin can get awkward. What holds us together as friends is the mutual understanding that what's more awkward than conversations about sin is pretending that it doesn't exist.

If I find that I cannot bear the thought of confessing my sins to my husband or a trusted friend, then I have a misunderstanding of who I am, who God is, and what Christ has accomplished on the cross.

Repentance Changes Everything

I wonder if someone just popped into your mind when you read about friends confessing their sins to one another. Perhaps you thought of a dear friend whom you are thankful for that you can talk with about your sin. Or maybe you thought of someone who would never "go there" with you. Or, you would never go there with her.

A life that is characterized by repentance changes a person. When your life is marked by ongoing repentance of sin and clinging to the grace of Jesus Christ, it makes other people want to do the same thing. They want to bring their burden to you so you'll share it with them and point them to the cross.

Free from the enslaving power of sin, the love of Christ wells up in us and powerfully energizes us to love others just as he has loved us (John 13:34). "In this is love, not that we have loved God but that he loved us and sent his Son to be the propitiation for our sins. Beloved, if God so loved us, we also ought to love one another" (1 John 4:10–11). Milton Vincent summarized these passages in this way: "So how can I come to love God with all of my being? The Bible teaches that genuine love in my heart for God is generated by an awareness of His love for me, and nowhere is the love of God more clearly revealed than in the gospel."[2]

With the help and encouragement of other Christians, we recognize afresh our need for the grace shown to us at the cross, and we repent of our sin. The fruit of repentance is sweet, and we're not the only ones who get to enjoy it. As the expulsive power of a renewed affection for Christ fills us more and more, his love spills over into our relationships with others. The *nations* get to see the glory of God on display in our love for one another!

So What?

Perhaps you're saying to yourself, "I get that. I totally get that. But what does this have to do with my loneliness for friendships?"

People who have ever been estranged from a friend or a spouse understand that the chasm between you seems impassable, and the tension is tangible. Clinging to the love of God in the gospel is also the only way that we can withstand the searing pain of deep-seated, soul-level hurts that can occur in the context of friendships among sinners on this side of heaven. Only persons who have tasted and know the grace of God in Christ are able to face this pain and come out of the experience praising God.

Romans 12:9–10 says, "Let love be genuine. Abhor what is evil; hold fast to what is good. Love one another with brotherly affection. Outdo one another in showing honor."

But thanks be to God, whose love covers a multitude of sins and motivates us to love one another earnestly! God will not throw my sin back into my face as a barrier to my blood-bought relationship as his daughter. "Sing aloud, O daughter of Zion; shout, O Israel! Rejoice and exult with all your heart, O daughter of Jerusalem! The LORD has taken away the judgments against you" (Zeph. 3:14–15).

Our loneliness can be helped by God's grace as we fix our eyes on Jesus. Jesus sets us free from things like the quest for comparison and all the judgmental gossip that goes with it. Jesus frees us to *love* as we have been loved with the love of God. Eager to share God's love with others, we make the sacrifices we need to make in order to arrange our schedule to accommodate relationships. As we go about the day, the Holy Spirit helps us to see the glimpses of grace in our lives and in the lives of others.

This brings us joy, and our feelings of entitlement fade away like the moon disappears in the morning. When we sin against our friends and the Spirit brings it to light, we choose to bask in that light. Instead of burying ourselves in a closet of shame, we step into the light of grace at the cross and repent. By God's grace, relationships are restored and strengthened.

Yes indeed, the gospel is undeniably relevant to our loneliness for friendships.

11

Treasure in Jars of Clay, Not in Fine Bone China

In the name of simplicity I bought a set of white porcelain serving dishes when we moved into our current home. They would probably not clash with the decorations for any particular occasion, and I am personally self-conscious about my inability to coordinate things, from dishes to clothes and accessories. I figured that those simple serving dishes could pass as classy, even if they were purchased for utilitarian purposes.

Peanut Butter Sandwiches on a Footed-Crystal Cake Stand

Along with the set of serving dishes I also bought a crystal pedestal cake stand that I only bring out for cakes. This stand is special; I keep it in its original box stuffed with crumpled paper and cardboard to keep it safe. This stand is unique; it only makes an appearance about once a month, whereas the common serving dishes are used on an ongoing basis. The serving dishes regularly disappear from our kitchen to be returned later, and I don't break a sweat. I can just use a different serving dish, but there's only one precious cake stand.

Even the children know that it's special. When I suggested one day at lunch that we lace our peanut butter sandwiches with pink sprinkles and eat them off of the cake stand, their eyes widened and they squealed with delight. You just don't eat sandwiches off a crystal cake stand, especially with a couple of kids who have butterfingers!

I'll admit that it took some guts for me to suggest that we eat our lunch off of a fancy piece of crystal. My kids are still in the plasticware phase of life and can barely be trusted with cups that don't have screw-top lids!

As I enjoyed my girls' delight in lunging for pink, sprinkle-laced sandwiches, I was also keenly aware of my nervousness over the situation. Then my two-year-old bumped the crystal lid a few inches away, and I heard the glass scrape on the countertop. Yikes. Surely if I called off our fancy lunch plans, then there would have been a protest involving tears and hiccups. Thankfully our lunch went without any incidents, but I haven't tried a stunt like that since then!

My reticence over sharing my crystal cake stand is in stark contrast to God's attitude about his children carrying the gospel to the ends of the earth. The life-giving gospel is glorious, precious, and powerful, and we are fragile jars of clay. It is no accident that God has chosen to entrust us with such a treasure.

> For what we proclaim is not ourselves, but Jesus Christ as Lord, with ourselves as your servants for Jesus' sake. For God, who said, "Let light shine out of darkness," has shone in our hearts to give the light of the knowledge of the glory of God in the face of Jesus Christ. But we have this treasure in jars of clay, to show that the surpassing power belongs to God and not to us. (2 Cor. 4:5–7)

The power of the gospel belongs to God and not to us. When God entrusts the gospel to us, it makes his power all the more obvious. God delights in glorifying himself by using jars of clay to show that the surpassing power of the gospel is his, and his alone.

But sometimes we'd much rather it be the other way around. We don't like to be weak. We prefer to be strong. We deny our weaknesses and failures and cover them up with pretense and excuses.

For many of us homemakers our greatest fear is in being found incompetent, insufficient, and ineffective. We prefer to look like we've got it all together. We give lip service to the idea that nobody's perfect, but we would rather die trying to prove that we're the exception to the rule.

One way to know if you might struggle with this is to listen to what your heart is saying next time you hear the doorbell ring. *Ding dong.* Perhaps your heart panics like mine does: "Oh! My friend is here. There's a dirty diaper on the coffee table. Quick! Throw it away. Eek! I'm wearing a T-shirt and sweat pants. Quick! Put on something that adults wear when they're trying to play grown-up."

In this chapter we're going to dig into the issues of authenticity, brokenness, and God's zeal for displaying his power through redeemed people who have a love/hate relationship with their sin.

We Would Rather Be Worshiped

God joyfully puts the treasure of the gospel into our clumsy, butterfinger hands despite our sinfulness, inadequacies, and failings. But sometimes we just don't buy that. Two main reasons come to mind.

First, it is contrary to our natural logic that God would choose to use the foolish and the weak to show himself to be wise. We have difficulty seeing how God is praised through our insufficiencies.

Wouldn't the Lord be more glorified through a flawlessly planned and executed hospitality event? Wouldn't the Lord's name be more honored if we knew how to articulate his goodness with enthusiastic clarity? Wouldn't it give more praise to our heavenly Father when his children look presentable and don't have any unsightly blemishes? Wouldn't the Creator be praised even more if his redeemed were admired the world over and lifted up as spectacular specimens of humanity?

We find it difficult to comprehend how God chooses to use the weak and broken to show himself to be strong and sufficient.

Second, we're uncomfortable with our weaknesses and failures. We would much rather host flawlessly planned and executed hospitality events. We'd prefer to articulate ourselves with clarity. We work so hard to look presentable and defer the effects of aging. We want to be admired.

Our preference boils down to just that—*we* are the ones who want to be admired. We want to live for our own glory. We're sinful, self-centered, and reluctant to worship God as our creator who has the right to do with us as he pleases.

When we are reluctant to exalt God and recognize his position of authority in our lives, we resent his desire to use us in our fragile, sinful states.

The Bad News I Believed

This posture of rebellion against our creator God gives room for false gospels. It's actually a misnomer to call something a "false gospel," since gospel means "good news." A false gospel is no gospel at all—it's bad news.

One of the pieces of bad news circulating out there in the world that I am particularly tempted to believe is that God is obligated to give you the life you want if you believe in him. And conversely, if you have the life you want, then it is a sign that God approves of you.

I've discussed in a previous chapter how my husband has dealt with chronic pain in his hands and arms for the duration of half of our marriage and our children's entire lives. I cannot count the number of nights I've awakened to feed one of our babies only to find my husband pacing the floor in the dark in agony—the agony of searing nerve pain and emotional distress. Watching him suffer, I would ask God, "Why, Lord?" Sometimes I would even make a mental list of all the earthly reasons why Dave shouldn't have to suffer like this: he's so young, he's got his whole life ahead of him, he wants to serve Jesus, he needs his arms, I need his arms, he hasn't done anything to deserve this, I haven't done anything to deserve this. Have you ever made a list like this when you're disturbed by some circumstances in your life?

When I believed that my circumstances were a result of the measure of my faith, I doubted the sincerity of my faith and the veracity of my prayers. These doubts were symptomatic of a deeper issue: ultimately I was questioning God's character. All kinds of questions stemmed from a misunderstanding of and lack of belief in who God is. Is God really as good as his Word says he is? Is God really willing to heal my husband? Is my faith in Jesus's work on the cross enough to guarantee that my prayers are heard in heaven? Did we commit some sin that wasn't covered by the cross so that we were being punished? Was there a better way to pray to make our prayers more effective?

The true gospel of grace shone brilliant light into these questions that I asked in the middle of those dark nights. I began to cling to the truth that God's character is unchanging and his power is immutable. The gospel is the lens through which God sees us when we have faith in his Son—the gospel is our one great, permanent circumstance. God is good if he relieves Dave of his pain. God is good if he doesn't. God's character remains unchanging.

There is one Mediator between man and God—the incarnate Son of God Jesus Christ. He is risen from the dead and is reigning at the Father's right hand, interceding for me even now. His blood speaks for me, so my prayers are heard in the throne room of heaven. I don't have to pray louder, longer, or more fervently in order for God to hear me better. Jesus's blood and righteousness is sufficient for me and gives me bold access to God's throne room. Of course, I will continue to pray that God will restore Dave's arms to healthy, functioning arms so that he can give me bear hugs again, twirl his preschool princesses in their nighties, and teach his son how to wrestle and throw an American football.

I spent so much wasted time and energy in denial that God could use our jars-of-clay lives. I needed a biblically informed view of who God is, and I needed to be open to the question that God had for me. Perhaps this is the same question God is asking you: "Are you willing to honor me in your brokenness?"

Lying Is a Symptom of Our Brokenness

Many of us may not be able to point to chronic pain or some other extreme circumstance in our lives to illustrate our brokenness or punctuate our struggles with living authentically. People may not be able to look at the trappings of your life and identify the ways in which you are weak, insufficient, or just plain messed up. But there isn't a single one of us who doesn't sense that nagging feeling that we just don't measure up—to God's standards, to the world's standards, to our friends' standards, to our family's standards, to our spouse's standards, or even to our own standards.

Lying to other people is just one of the symptoms by which we show our need for a Savior. Lying to our friends is especially indicative of our brokenness. Do you ever lie to your friends? Of course we don't mean to lie when we follow social protocol and answer "Fine" to someone's "How are you today?" Of course we don't intentionally walk into a room with the hopes of misleading everyone we talk to. *Or do we?*

Perhaps our relationships are terminally casual because we're not willing to disclose what's at the heart level. Perhaps nobody dares to ask. Maybe we're unsure of how we are really doing. Maybe we're not willing to hear from others how they are really doing. Maybe we're afraid of the truth—that it would overwhelm us. Maybe we're insecure because we've been burned in the past. Maybe we're selfishly absorbed with what goes on in our own hearts. Maybe we're just ignorant to the beauty of self-disclosure shared for the sake of the gospel. Maybe we'd rather cling to our assumptions of others.

Sometimes we're so wrapped up in our own pretenses that recognizing the real us is difficult. Sometimes even *we* aren't sure how we are doing. Sure, we may be polished and neat on the outside—we forget nothing, we're prepared for anything (how full is your purse?), not a hair is out of place, our living room looks like nobody lives in it. But on the inside there's a messy, disheveled soul staggering under the weight of the façade we're building.

We want to look good in front of others, and we want to look good in front of ourselves, too. Someone once said, "A lie is a stab into the very vitals of the body of Christ." If we are members of one body, how can one member lie to or deceive another? How can we weep with those who weep and rejoice with those who rejoice if we are ignorant of the pain and joy in one another's lives?

When the facade I construct for my heart overflows into my home, I turn homemaking into a grandiose display of my personal style. I forget that homemaking is not primarily about my personality; it is primarily to adorn the gospel because the grace of God has appeared, bringing salvation for all people (Titus 2:11).

Jesus Is Our Greatest Reality

Jesus is the most real person who ever lived. There was not one gram of pretense in him. He never pretended to be anything he was not. He is our firm foundation, and we are confident because we are in him. We are bold because he has gone before us. We persevere through trials because he is interceding for us. We declare his victory over our sin because he has nailed the condemning record against us to the cross. When we sense that we are self-absorbed, preoccupied with what others think of us, and intimidated to be honest with others, we can find help in Christ.

Jesus is our Great High Priest who is sympathetic to our weaknesses. He knows how we are tempted, and he can help us stand firm and resist the lies of the Devil. Moreover, Jesus gives us his righteousness. There is hope for us who struggle with timidity and pretense. There is hope for us who forget on a daily basis the work of Christ on the cross.

When we realize that we've blown it yet again, we must throw ourselves at the mercy of God shown to us at the cross. When our attitudes are poor, we must cry out to Jesus for help. When we're certain that we're doing fine and the shroud of pretense begins to envelop us, we must repent of our pride and grab hold of Jesus, confident that he will heal our broken hearts.

The grace of God reminds us to live in the reality of the gospel and the future that he has promised to us in Christ. Our confidence comes from what Jesus has done and will do in the future in raising us from the dead to eternal life, just as he was raised. We can reject the self-love of self-loathing and prideful gloating. This will happen when we see Jesus as he truly is. In seeing him truly, he becomes more and more precious to us, and we in turn become shaped by him as we behold him (2 Cor. 3:18).

What about When You Put This Book Down?

These truths are lovely to read and meditate on right now, but what about ten minutes from now? How sturdy are these truths when you have to make a decision whether to answer that phone call or when you walk into a room of people? The sturdiness and trustworthiness of the gospel is only as sure and certain as God. Listen to what God says about himself:

> Know therefore that the LORD your God is God, the faithful God who keeps covenant and steadfast love with those who love him and keep his commandments, to a thousand generations. (Deut. 7:9)

> The Rock, his work is perfect, for all his ways are justice. A God of faithfulness and without iniquity, just and upright is he. (Deut. 32:4)

> For your steadfast love is great to the heavens,
>   your faithfulness to the clouds. (Ps. 57:10)

> O LORD God of hosts,
>   who is mighty as you are, O LORD,
>   with your faithfulness all around you? (Ps. 89:8)

> God is faithful, by whom you were called into the fellowship of his Son, Jesus Christ our Lord. (1 Cor. 1:9)

> He who calls you is faithful; he will surely do it. (1 Thess. 5:24)

> Let us hold fast the confession of our hope without wavering, for he who promised is faithful. (Heb. 10:23)

Faith believes God. Faith believes that we are who God says we are. Faith believes what Christ has done on the cross. Faith believes that God will fulfill his promises to us. That is the kind of faith that changes a person.

Jars of Clay Exulting in God

Living in the reality of this gospel by faith *will* motivate you to love others as Jesus loves. This afternoon at that dreaded social gathering, or tonight when you spend time with your spouse and have a difficult conversation, or tomorrow morning when you open your home to some friends or strangers—you must be confident that what Jesus promises you in the future will come to pass. He has promised to be with you, even to the end of the age. Jesus has promised you himself, and he will give you everything you need for life and godliness.

You can trust Jesus because he died for you! Romans 8:32 says, "He who did not spare his own Son but gave him up for us all, how will he not also with him graciously give us all things?"

When you can't see any way out of a situation because you lack the skills, expertise, or knowledge, but God has called you to serve, trust God. Move forward with the confidence that God loves to do things to demonstrate his power. "Not by might, nor by power, but by my Spirit, says the Lord of hosts" (Zech. 4:6).

When you're in a conversation with someone who needs to know the truth about Jesus, trust God. Believe God is powerful when he calls you to proclaim Jesus Christ as Lord and yourself a servant for his sake (2 Cor. 4:5).

If you're feeling intimidated by someone's academic arguments or strong personality, trust God. Believe God is wise when he calls you in your weakness and fear to proclaim the truth about Jesus Christ and him. Don't rely on the wisdom of men, but let your faith rest in God as the Holy Spirit demonstrates his power (1 Cor. 2:1–5).

When you're lacking confidence in what God has called you to do, and you're considering turning back because of fear of failure or inadequacy, trust God. Treasure God's supremacy as you walk by faith and take captive every thought to obey Christ (2 Cor. 10:4–5).

If you're looking over your broken life and wondering, "What on earth am I even doing for God?" trust God. Hold on tight to grace-besotted statements from Paul, like, "My grace is sufficient for you, for my power is made perfect in weakness." Then boast in your weaknesses so that the power of Christ rests on you. Be content that when you are weak in those moments, you are strong in Christ (2 Cor. 12:9–10).

God is delighted to use fragile jars of clay and our imperfect homes for the sake of his fame among the nations!

12

The Idol of a Picture-Perfect Home

A few years ago my friend Samantha did our family's laundry for over six weeks. No, she didn't lose a bet, and yes, I did have a washing machine. Yes, I am a bit lazy with the laundry sometimes, and Samantha is a servant-hearted person. Plus, she folds undershirts so much better than I do. Oh, and the detergent she was using at the time smelled wonderful. But that's not why she walked to our apartment (from her nearby apartment) carrying our clothes back and forth for over six weeks.

This all goes back to the way our apartment building was designed. The building went up rather quickly, and it was built entirely out of cement. Among other issues, it contracted while being built too fast, so the pipes were not flushed of the incidental cement dust that had settled inside.

Image Is Everything

When we moved into the brand-new apartment, we had the movers connect the washing machine to the appropriate pipes. In the first running of the machine we knew there was a problem. What do you get when you mix cement dust with water? That's right—a pipe full of cement. I suppose I ought to have been grateful that the pipes to the toilet were not full of cement, too. If that had been the case, we would have given up on the repairmen coming over and just moved in with Samantha and her husband!

I began calling the building maintenance crew on a regular basis, begging them to come and replace the pipe. Apparently so did many of my neighbors, as one by one they discovered that their brand-new apartment wasn't so perfect after all.

But the maintenance crew had other things to worry about than our building's pipes. As a result of having massive plumbing issues, **it** had developed the telltale signs of internal issues, as unsightly cracks and water stains started appearing on the outside of the building.

For six weeks I called the maintenance help desk and asked for a repairman to come remove the old pipe and replace it with one that was cement-free, but to no avail. My neighbors did the same. The water stains on the paint outside the building, however, got loads of special care and attention. Because of the water leaking from cement-laden pipes, new stains appeared every week. And every week the maintenance crew showed up to paint over the new water stains and fill in the cracks. The side of the building facing the road was always painted first.

I was mildly annoyed the first time I saw them painting over the stains. Then I was livid the fourth time the painters were out patching up the exterior walls. I stood outside the building glaring up at the repairmen on the scaffolding while I called the helpdesk and tried my best to keep my cool. "The pipes *inside* are still *broken*. They will keep *leaking* unless you fix the pipes. Please, we do not care about the paint. Ple-e-e-e-ease send them *inside* to fix the *pipes*."

This scenario reminded me of what one of my local friends said: "Your culture says, 'Don't judge a book by its cover.' We think that's silly! Of course you must judge a book by its cover. How else will you know if it is a good book?"

In this case the exterior presentation of the building was more important than the functionality of its inner workings and the contentment of the tenants. The painters continued to diligently beautify the exterior walls while the plumbers were delayed. A landscaping crew even came by in the meantime to rip up wilting flowers and replace them with vibrant new ones. Image is everything.

We're not so different from the diligent painters. We work so hard to build an image in our home that we often neglect the inner workings that define and shape the home. And when things are not functioning well inside our home, the issues seep out into the open where everyone can see. When this happens, our instinct is to patch up the cracks and paint over the stains to the neglect of fixing the inside.

But the gospel leads us into the truth and enables us to dare to uncover what lies beneath the beautifully manicured surface of our lives.

The Gutsy Grace of the Gospel

When I was a kid I watched the movie *The NeverEnding Story* a few too many times. In one scene a sage is talking with Atreyu the warrior's companion, a Luck Dragon named Falkor. He says the next test the warrior Atreyu must pass is the Magic Mirrorgate, in which he must stand before a mirror and see his "true self." Falkor says, "So what? That won't be too hard for him." The sage replies, "Oh, that's what everyone thinks! But kind people find out that they are cruel. Brave men discover that they are really cowards! Confronted by their true selves, most men run away *screaming!*"

In the light of the gospel we can have the determination to face what we really are and not run away screaming. Jesus faced our sin and our enemy and determined to remain on the cross until our debt for every last sin was paid in full. He nailed the record of condemnation against us to the cross in triumph!

Through Jesus we can face up to who we really are in contrast to the image we would prefer to display for others. The gospel inspires in us a willingness to cede control to God over the image we are trying to portray through our lives in the home. Through Jesus we can be most concerned with imaging God and being conformed to his image. Because of the gospel we can run away from any Magic Mirrorgate, rejoicing in who God is instead of devastated by who we are.

Style and Preference

Homemakers all have their own way of doing things. This much is obvious anytime you walk into someone else's home and notice the differences and similarities to yours. Sometimes these preferences can fit into a specific mold or stereotype, and for the rest of us, "eclectic" is a label we wear proudly. All sorts of labels describe homemakers these days—vintage, green, simple, shabby chic, modern, homemade, and the list goes on.

God designed each of us to have different preferences for the way we manage and design our homes. One mother of three whom I know has a shoe rack in her home's mudroom that has laminated name cards on each of the spaces where family members place their shoes. Another friend with three children feels stifled by systems of organization like these and describes the pile of shoes in her kids' closet as a "shoe free-for-all." Both women are quite content with the way this works for their families.

Living overseas I have the opportunity to be entertained in homes of people from cultures that differ vastly from my own. Noting different styles of living rooms has been somewhat of a hobby of mine. In one friend's home the living room looks like she picked up a catalog and said, "This one. This is the room I want. I'll take everything on this page and have it set up exactly how I see it in this picture." Another friend's home has a relatively empty-looking living room suited only with couches on the floor and a rug in the middle. Another friend's living room appears as though every member of the family lives in it—with telltale signs of an active family life scattered around the room. Each of these homemakers would say the priority of serving people is the reason her living room is arranged and managed the way it is. Their personal preferences are also part of it, as their style is a beautiful and creative form of self-expression.

The priority of service is certainly true for Christians. The purpose of a home is to serve the people who live there and the strangers who are invited in. Homemaking as unto the Lord is an adornment of the glorious gospel!

Idols of the Home

But because our hearts are idol factories, as John Calvin famously said, as we manage our homes we are prone to carving idols out of the same resources that God intends for us to use to worship him instead.

Not making an idol out of our homes is tricky. I've personally experienced what it feels like to be obsessed with the idea of organization in my home. I thought I was being driven by the maxim "God is a God of order and not of chaos." I thought that if everything had a place, then my heart would feel at peace because strict orderliness is godly. But instead of worshiping God, I just wanted to be in control. I was worshiping my image and thought it wouldn't be so bad if others admired me, too.

Other homemakers may have a different vice. Perhaps it is the idea of your home being your sanctuary.

I've also had struggles with the idol of self-expression, seeing my home primarily as an extension of myself. If something was out of place or not just so, then I felt it reflected poorly on my personhood or character. Again I was serving my own image—not God's.

Praise the Lord that there is hope for homemakers like us who are so easily distracted by idols and prone to propagating our own image.

The Conspiracy against You

We need to recognize that the Devil has laid out traps to ensnare us. The traps are webs of lies surrounding who God is, who you are, and what Christ has done for you. When you get entangled in this web of lies, you get tripped up and your spiritual limbs get so stiff that you feel paralyzed when you are called to walk by faith.

Don't be a victim of identity theft. Learn what the truth looks like so that you can recognize these traps. Don't assume things about God's character or his intentions. Read the Scriptures and meditate on what it says about who God is. Don't presume that what the world says about you is true. In the Bible you can discover the reason God made you and how he designed you.

Be wary when something presents itself as "the way, the truth, and the life" and entices you to follow. Don't be a sucker when you see advertisements that are designed to make you feel that you need to buy into their image in order to be "the you that you always wanted to be." Go back to the Scriptures as your authority that proclaims that Jesus is *the* way, *the* truth, and *the* life (John 14:6).

Our Gospel Identity

Christian, everything God has for you is grace upon grace because of what Jesus has done for you. To us depraved sinners who are the least deserving, Jesus gave his life. He cherished God's law perfectly, which is something we would never do. Jesus loved God's law, and he fulfilled God's perfect law by obeying God perfectly. No one could have done this except Jesus, the sinless one. He then gave us his life by dying as our substitute. On the cross he took our sins onto himself and allowed the Father to pour out his wrath upon him. Our sins have been paid in full because of Jesus's sacrifice, so there is now no condemnation for those who are in Christ Jesus (Rom. 8:1).

Jesus gave his life in our place as a substitute for sin. We are forgiven. In Christ we are not just forgiven and given a blank slate so we can start over and try to live good and holy lives. No! We don't have a blank slate to start over and get a "second chance." If God gave us a second chance to live perfectly or even a two-millionth chance to walk in perfect holiness before him, we would still blow it. Jesus gives us his life of righteousness when we are justified by faith in him. The record of sin against us was nailed to the cross, and Jesus gives us his record of perfect righteousness.

Christian, this gospel is the reality in which you live this morning. God is absolutely free in his choice to set his love on whomever he pleases, and in Christ he chose you. You didn't deserve it, and that's the beauty and glory of grace upon grace.

Your image is not really about you but about him. God created you in his image, and he is about the work of redeeming you right there in the midst of your life in the home. Part of your image bearing and image conforming is experiencing the joy of making God your treasured possession, as he has made you his. Throw away all the self-images that denigrate your personhood by calling your homemaking an evolution of animal instinct. Seeing ourselves through any other lens is a slur on the cross and an insult to the worthiness of Jesus, who is worthy to receive the reward of his suffering, namely, worship from men and women from every tribe, tongue, people, and nation.

Practically Speaking, Imaging God in Your Home

What does life-changing faith look like on a day-to-day basis in the midst of the mundane? Simply put, faith looks backward and forward.

Faith looks backward to the cross and believes that Jesus has purchased every spiritual blessing for us with his blood (Eph. 1:3). Faith also looks forward to the reward of all that God has for us in Christ. This is the kind of faith that changes the way you live today and makes you into a homemaker whose goal and delight is in God and in being conformed to his image.

By faith we believe that God chose us in Christ in love to be adopted as God's children "according to the purpose of his will" (Eph. 1:4–5). Tomorrow morning we can get out of bed and confidently go straight to our Father to tell him that we love him and need him, and we can share with him everything that is on our hearts. Faith believes that God will satisfy us with joy forever.

By faith we believe that God created us in Christ Jesus for good works (Eph. 2:10). As we're making breakfast we can plan the day around serving others for the sake of the gospel, knowing that this is what God has created us to do. Furthermore, his divine power has granted to us all things that pertain to life and godliness because he has called us (2 Pet. 1:3). Faith believes that God has given the believer eternal life.

By faith we believe that God is building us up as a spiritual house, to be a holy priesthood, to offer spiritual sacrifices acceptable to him through Jesus (1 Pet. 2:5). At the first hint of inadequacy in our homemaking we can cling to our Great High Priest, who makes the deeds we do in faith acceptable to God. Faith believes that God will finish the work he has started in us (Phil. 1:6).

By faith we believe that we have been brought near to God by the blood of Christ, whereas we had been far off and without hope (Eph. 2:13). As we go about our errands for the home, we can initiate friendships with strangers and invite them into our home because we're no longer strangers in God's house but citizens—even sons and daughters (Eph. 2:19). Faith believes that God will bring us into his home.

By faith we believe that we have been reconciled to God and to one another through the cross (Eph. 2:16). At the first sign of temptation to make our home an idol, we can focus on God's delight in gathering together a people for the praise of his name—a dwelling place for God by the Spirit (Eph. 2:22). Faith believes that God will be exalted in all the earth.

By faith we believe that God will give us the courage we need to share the gospel in the face of opposition (1 Thess. 2:2). We can manage our homes tonight in grace and love despite living in a world that is hostile to the gospel and seeks to destroy what God loves. Faith believes that God will overthrow the Devil and destroy his works (2 Thess. 2:8).

Set Apart Your Home for Jesus

Jesus is the true and better image, as he is the image of the invisible God (Col. 1:15). Jesus created all things in heaven and on earth—all things were created through him and for him (Col. 1:16). Jesus is before all things, and in him all things hold together (Col. 1:17). Jesus is the sovereign Lord over every square centimeter in your home—from the pipes to the television to the mattresses. He is Lord over it, and he desires that you use what he's given you to glorify him. That doesn't mean that your home needs to be perfect by the world's standards or even by your own personal standards, but consecrated by God's standards.

In Romans 12:1–2 we see a description of what it means to set ourselves apart for God: "I appeal to you therefore, brothers, by the mercies of God, to present your bodies as a living sacrifice, holy and acceptable to God, which is your spiritual worship. Do not be conformed to this world, but be transformed by the renewal of your mind, that by testing you may discern what is the will of God, what is good and acceptable and perfect." Since Jesus is Lord over all things and God is subjecting all things under his feet (1 Cor. 15:27), including our homes, by his grace we use our homes to worship him.

13

Does Contentment in Christ Come with a Nap?

"Mommy-y-y-y! The baby has your pho-o-o-ne!" my daughter's voice drifted down the hallway.

"How'd he manage to do that?" I wondered aloud. He must have unplugged my phone from the charging cable on the nightstand next to his crib. I dropped the sheets on the bed I was making to go rescue my phone. In my mind's eye I could see the baby drool seeping into that tiny hole where you plug in the headphones and shorting out the speakers.

As Serious as a Diaperless Baby

When I stepped into the room and saw him, I gasped. "Oh no! No!"

Sure enough, there he was holding my phone in his chubby little hand. What took my breath away was what I saw in his other hand. He was holding a diaper. *His* diaper.

His happy squealing told me that he was quite proud of his new trick. I frantically patted around the crib and his blanket—dry! Thankfully the drafty air hadn't gotten to him yet. I felt a wave of relief wash over me. This is the kind of mercy that you don't appreciate until you find out the peril you were in.

I was specifically thankful for two things at the same time. I was glad that my daughter let me know that the baby was about to use my phone for his mischief making. If she hadn't sounded the alarm, then who knows how many prank calls he could have placed to the last number I dialed. I was also glad to intervene in the more urgent issue. Namely, his little bottom was freewheeling diaper-free.

Obviously both the stolen mobile phone and the baby's bare bottom required my attention. But my daughter had focused only on the first issue of importance. She neglected to tell me about the more urgent matter.

Sometimes we read the Bible that way. We read something important and fixate on it to the neglect of other things that are just as important or sometimes even more urgent.

We Tend to Ignore Contentment

As we read the Bible, we may come across a passage that contains several important issues. We might meditate on one issue, prayerfully consider it, and discuss it with others. When we think we understand that one important thing, we often move on to another passage, passing by the other issues.

This is unfortunate, because we stand to gain tremendous benefit from persisting in prayerful meditation on passages of Scripture. As we focus our minds and hearts to understand the Word of God, the Holy Spirit will continue to illumine it and write it indelibly on our hearts. Every once in a while as we're reading the Bible we might not notice something as serious and urgent as a diaper-less baby, but sometimes we might.

The apostle Paul's example of contentment is a case in point. How many times have we heard this verse cited? "Not that I am speaking of being in need, for I have learned in whatever situation I am to be content" (Phil. 4:11). Contentment is one of those desirable things that we all want to have yet rarely feel as though we have it. That's why Philippians 4:11 seems like a nice verse to write on a sticky note to post inside your closet to remind you of your abundant wealth when you think, "I've got *nothing* to wear!"

Some of us who are more cynical than others (myself included) might be tempted to scoff and say, "Paul says he is content in whatever situation? Obviously he wasn't in *my* situation." Honestly, I don't go around asking my friends to quote Philippians 4:11 to me when I'm shopping or in the throes of self-pity because of my circumstances.

Should We Just Throw It All Away?

We all want to learn contentment, but we don't always enjoy the *learning* part. Most times we would much rather have God wave a magic wand over our heads.

Contentment is elusive and widely desired by everyone—not just Christians. Some world religions hold out simplicity and asceticism as the solution to discontentment. Vain materialism is an attempt to achieve contentment. Where we live, we are witness to some of the world's most extreme pursuits of contentment through sheer buying power.

For me, as I go about my day in my home, I can see how attempting minimalism and simplicity seems like the solution to my discontent. When I glance into my children's room after I've asked them to clean up, and I see piles of books strewn all over the place, the play jewelry has been dumped onto someone's bed, and tiny chunks of crusted Play-Doh litter the floor, I feel a tremendous lack of peace.

The clutter bothers me, so I start lobbing vain threats into the atmosphere: "If these toys don't get put away properly, I'll assume you don't want them anymore, and I'll throw them into the garbage." I might make a mental note of the things I need to organize better. If only I had that particular closet available or a more efficient system for storing toys, school supplies, clothes, *whatever*—then I'd be happy.

I think that if I don't see any chaos, then that assumes the presence of peace. That's the deluding lie. I humbly submit to you, if your heart is anything like mine, it doesn't matter how well you've organized your storage closet, your kids' toys, or your in-box if there is discontent bound up in your heart.

If there is discontent bound up in your heart, then there is no room in your house where you can go and feel peace. You will, as I have, attempt to create the perfect environment that is rid of distractions so that you can focus. At the end of the day you will find out that the chaos isn't your environment—it's in your heart.

The Diaperless Baby in Philippians 4:11

Christian contentment is about so much more than being happy with what you're wearing or the size of your savings account or the aesthetic quality of your home.

We'll look first to the most obvious point of Philippians 4:11. The most apparent thing we notice is Paul's experience of contentment. That is, he has learned contentment *regardless* of what his circumstances are. He is writing this letter to the Philippians while he is in jail, chained to guards, and imprisoned for preaching the gospel. He is near the end of his life and most likely in a great deal of physical pain as a result of the many beatings he endured over the years. I can't imagine that the prison catering company or the inmate urgent-care clinic were very accommodating to Paul.

Yet Paul says he has learned to be content in *any* circumstance. What initially stands out to us is the broad, sweeping extremity of his statement—"*whatever* situation." The Bible is God's inerrant Word, so we can be assured that "whatever situation" doesn't mean "most situations" or "just the situations I enjoy" or "only the situations I control." Paul says he has learned contentment in *whatever* situation.

When I read that statement, I'm humbled. Here's Paul, content in chains. And here's me—ready to complain about things like the Internet that is too slow and precious children who woke me before I was ready to get up. "Get a grip, you wimp," I rebuke myself. "Look at Paul! You've got nothing to complain about. Paul has on chains and he's happy, and you're not even happy with the new shoes you bought."

But Philippians 4:11 isn't just a correction to ungrateful, privileged people. It isn't just a correction to ungrateful, less-privileged people either. This first portion of the verse, while astounding and life-changing, is just the tip of the iceberg, so to speak. That part of the verse is like the mobile phone that the bare-bottomed baby is chewing on.

Let's look again. Philippians 4:11 is also useful for training in righteousness. The Greek word Paul uses for *content* means "self-sufficient." *What did he just say?* Paul is *self*-sufficient? Self-sufficiency sounds quite odd and off-kilter to the Christian ear that has been trained to listen for things that pronounce and extol the sufficiency of Christ.

What Paul Means by Self-Sufficiency

How can Paul say that he has learned to be self-sufficient? Everything about the idea of self-sufficiency seems to fly in the face of the gospel in which we are saved by grace that is not from ourselves.

Paul certainly lived in the reality of this gospel of grace, so he clearly cannot be casting a shadow of doubt on the sufficiency of Christ. By no means! Paul is *affirming* that the grace of Christ he experiences in his life is sufficient to satisfy his heart in any and every circumstance. His experience of grace is something he carries within himself as the Holy Spirit indwells him. Jeremiah Burroughs explains, "Because he had a right to the covenant and promise, which virtually contains everything, and an interest in Christ, the fountain and good of all, it is no marvel that he said that in whatsoever state he was in, he was content."[1]

If this is true of the apostle Paul—that his experience of grace is something he carries within himself as the Holy Spirit indwells him—then as children of God who cling to the same gospel Paul preached, it is true for us too.

If the same Holy Spirit indwells us, then we can learn contentment. I love how Burroughs describes this learning: "Contentment in every condition is a great art, a spiritual mystery. It is to be learned, and to be learned as a mystery."[2] A great art and a spiritual mystery! Burroughs is saying that contentment doesn't come by a mathematical formula or an alignment of optimal circumstances. We can't just insert the right amount of currency into a vending machine and push a button to receive contentment. We can't just furnish the perfect living room or simplify our lifestyle in just the right way. There is no mystical pattern to follow, no number of prayers to recite, no quota of paying it forward to complete. If our journey of learning contentment is a piece of artwork, then God himself is the artist.

There is no magic bullet for perfect contentment in Christ unless that bullet is one that sends you home to Jesus, where you will be perfectly content in his presence forever.

Night Weaning and Contentment

One of my favorite things about reading the Puritans is how they connected the mundane moments of life to God's great work of making us holy. Burroughs wrote an entire book on content-ment, which includes a lesson in wisdom, including this glimpse of grace:

> So, when God would wean you from some outward comforts in this world, oh, how fretting and discontented you are! Children will not sleep themselves nor let their mothers sleep when they are weaning; and so, when God would wean us from the world, and we fret, vex, and murmur, this is a childish spirit.

He is *not* kidding. On either point. Burroughs may have lived in the 1600s, but he might as well have been at our breakfast table this morning.

When a child is weaning and venturing into solid foods, there can be a great learning curve. My youngest child eats every meal like he's the littlest kid at the kid table at Thanksgiving who has to grab the sweet potatoes before the biggest cousin takes it all. My son is just one year old, yet he eats so fast that he stuffs his cheeks like a chipmunk, then cries that the food doesn't go down to his belly fast enough. His god is his stomach, so to speak. If his belly is full, then he feels content. What an incredible illustration we can see here. When we're learning the art of Christian contentment, we're not so different from babies transitioning from drinking milk to eating solid foods. We're used to consuming our food quite easily—it is liquid, after all. But when we're called upon to mature and feed ourselves and chew our food, we balk at the hard work.

Submission to God Is Primary to Contentment

Burroughs gives practical advice for those who seek contentment but struggle with where to start: "Exercise faith by often resigning yourself to God, by giving yourself up to God and his ways. The more you in a believing way surrender up yourself to God, the more quiet and peace you will have."[3] Here we see him connect contentment with submission to God, which is an entirely different approach from what the world would recommend. The world recommends manipulating your circumstances to achieve contentment. Earn more money to buy what you need and want. If your current spouse doesn't suit you, then find a way out of your marriage to find someone who makes you happy. There's the philanthropic strain that says to give away what you have to others to find happiness in your good deeds. Asceticism would advise you to get rid of whatever is distracting your soul from inner peace.

Christianity would have you submit to God so that he can give you contentment in him. Jesus clarifies this idea of submitting to God when he illustrates the alternatives. "No one can serve two masters, for either he will hate the one and love the other, or he will be devoted to the one and despise the other. You cannot serve God and money. Therefore I tell you, do not be anxious about your life" (Matt. 6:24–25). Jesus is speaking to a crowd of people who were not so different from you and me. They were not just mildly concerned about what they ate and drank and the clothes they wore—they were anxious. "What will we eat? What will we drink? What will we wear?" Jesus addresses the heart behind the questions. Three times in Matthew 6:25–34 the Lord says, "Do not be anxious." He explains the better way when he says, "But seek first the kingdom of God and his righteousness, and all these things will be added to you" (v. 33).

It takes a lot of pride to be anxious. When I'm anxious, I'm assuming that my being anxious and the knee-jerk reactions spawned by my anxiety are what's best for me. Seeking God's kingdom is not a path paved in anxiety but in peaceful submission. In other words, seeking God's kingdom is a directly related to our contentment.

Contentment Can't Come from Action Steps

I know this sounds way too hard. Submit to God in order to resolve discontentment? I would much rather believe a promise that ten-or-so easy steps to organizing my home will guarantee that the clutter of my life will disappear. In a sense, it is easier to make a plan of action steps to eliminate the chaos of your home. I'm a big fan of action steps. I've upgraded my to-do lists into a computer software program that organizes things better than I ever have. I've learned (the hard way) to delegate some responsibilities around the villa/parsonage.

Actions steps are good things! Reduce the number of trips you make to the grocery store by careful planning. Slim down your busy schedule by carpooling with others. Recycle your belongings into the hands of more needy people. Simplify your world with careful discipline and more sophisticated planning. These are all *very* good things.

But none of these "things to do" can deliver the peace they promise, especially if they become elevated to the status of an idol in our hearts.[4] I know firsthand that action steps are the easiest things to reach for. It does give me a temporary sense of relief knowing that at least I am doing something and not just wallowing in my discontented situation. It's a nice distraction to do something—anything—so long as it isn't sitting still and stewing in the spiritual chaos that I'm feeling.

Things to Do Always

But Paul says there is something we can do. Look at what Paul says a few verses back in Philippians 4:4: "Rejoice in the Lord always; again I will say, rejoice." You can put that on the top of your to-do list. But don't put it as a numerical "Things to do #1: Rejoice in the Lord." Put it at the very top, as in the highest, superseding priority you have in all things: "Rejoice in the Lord *always*." Rejoice in the Lord *as* you go about thing-to-do number one, number two, number three—you get the picture. Rejoicing in the Lord is primary to your contentment, because only the Lord can eternally and sufficiently satisfy your soul.

Only *agape* has the eternal remedy to our discontentment.

Don't Let Your Heart Turn Blessings into Idols

Learning the art of contentment involves thanking God for the things he's given us. Our gratitude to God for his blessings is a vehicle that God uses to give us something far more satisfying, namely, himself.

God is the giver of all good gifts (James 1:17) and he uses these gifts to raise our soul's affections to greater heights than any good thing in this world ever could. All of God's gifts serve this purpose—to raise our soul's affections for him. Consider the gift of forgiveness of sins. Even gratitude for something like the gift of forgiveness is shortsighted unless we see it as the vehicle that removes the obstacle of our sin, allowing us to enjoy enduring satisfaction in God.

The gift of God is greater than a spouse who accepts you despite your junk, greater than a child who loves you with enthusiastic affection, greater than popularity among your group of friends, greater than even the approval you give yourself when you like what you see in the mirror or what you've created to put on the dinner table.

One way that God's gifts can serve our eternal joy is through how these gifts help us interpret our cravings. Think of a gift from God. Have you got it in your mind? Now ask yourself, what is it about this particular gift that satisfies your soul, albeit temporarily? When you begin to see how a gift from God touches your soul, you'll notice that the gift is actually pointing at a space in your heart that God can fill eternally with an enduring joy. When we treasure God himself as the ultimate gift, the gifts he gives us become glasses through which we can see the sacred with clarity. When this happens, we can agree with the saints of old who adored God for who he is, "Oh give thanks to the LORD, for he is good; for his steadfast love endures forever!" (1 Chron. 16:34).

God Wants to Give You Himself

Sometimes my infant son is grumpy and discontented because we won't let him do what he wants to do more than anything else in the whole wide world. His favorite game at the moment is to try to stick his arm into a flushing toilet. The first time he did this, his face lit up with sheer delight. Now we know that he is not to be trusted with access to the bathroom. Whenever he enters a room, his sisters know that it is their critical duty to ensure that the bathroom door is shut. They are grossed out by his game just as much as I am.

But he is on to them, and he won't be deterred. Either he has a sixth sense or he is better at spotting the potty dance than I am, but whenever one of his sisters gets up to go to the bathroom, he is not far behind. Squealing, he will drop whatever he is doing and crawl like a speed racer to the bathroom—only to have the door shut in his face.

We ban the baby from the toilet because we love him. It's a terrible idea to stick your arm into a festering whirlpool of bacteria and filth! Additionally, it is a priority in our house to have privacy while you do your business. No amount of his crying and bellyaching from the other side of the bathroom door is enough. No one ever opens the door to let him in so he can put his arm into the noisy, swirling water. He doesn't know that what he thinks will make him happy will make him ill.

God is a good Father, and he never, ever considers for even

one moment letting us remain satisfied with anything less than himself, because he is the most satisfying treasure in the whole wide world. Psalm 37:4 says, "Delight yourself in the LORD, and he will give you the desires of your heart." When our delight is in the Lord, the desire of our heart *is the Lord.* God will most assuredly and gladly give you himself. After all, he's already demonstrated his commitment to freely giving himself to us for our eternal gladness. He sent his Son Jesus to die on the cross and remove every obstacle between us!

We see glimpses of God's grace in our homes when we cherish God through the gospel of Jesus Christ. The solution to our problems in the home *and* the impetus for our enjoyment of life in the home is fellowship with God through Christ Jesus's atoning sacrifice on the cross. Matthew 6:21 says, "For where your treasure is, there your heart will be also." May Jesus be our treasure as our lives are hidden in him.

Notes

Introduction

1. Augustine, "Letter 143 'To Marcellinus,'" *Letters 211–270: Works of Saint Augustine* (Hyde Park, NY: New City Press, 2005), 2.4.

Chapter 1: Today's Forecast

1. John Piper, "Honoring the Biblical Call of Motherhood," sermon, May 8, 2005.
2. Westminster Shorter Catechism, Question 1.
3. Milton Vincent, *A Gospel Primer for Christians: Learning to See the Glories of God's Love* (Bemidji, MN: Focus, 2008), 21.

Chapter 2: Don't Smurf the Gospel

1. Graeme Goldsworthy, *Gospel-Centered Hermeneutics: Foundations and Principles of Evangelical Biblical Interpretation* (Downers Grove, IL: IVP Academic, 2000).
2. One such book is Greg Gilbert's readable and concise *What Is the Gospel?* (Wheaton, IL: Crossway, 2010).
3. Timothy S. Lane and Paul David Tripp, *How People Change* (Greensboro, NC: New Growth Press, 2008), 5.
4. A helpful book to read on this topic is Trevin Wax's *Counterfeit Gospels: Rediscovering the Good News in a World of False Hope* (Chicago, IL: Moody, 2011).
5. Wendy Alsup, *Practical Theology for Women* (Wheaton, IL: Crossway, 2008), 26.
6. D. A. Carson, "What Is the Gospel?" in *For the Fame of God's Name: Essays in Honor of John Piper*, ed. D. A. Carson, Sam Storms, and Justin Taylor (Wheaton, IL: Crossway, 2010), 165.
7. J. Mack Stiles, *Marks of the Messenger: Knowing, Living, and Speaking the Gospel* (Downers Grove, IL: InterVarsity, 2010).

8. Carson, "What Is the Gospel?" 165.
9. Milton Vincent, *A Gospel Primer for Christians: Learning to See the Glories of God's Love* (Bemidji, MN: Focus, 2008), 13.
10. Martin Luther on Luke 22:7–20 (April 1534).

Chapter 4: Christ in You, the Hope of Glory

1. Richard Sibbes, *Glorious Freedom* (Carlisle, PA: Banner of Truth, 2000), 110.
2. Jonathan Edwards, "On Efficacious Grace," in *The Works of Jonathan Edwards* (Edinburgh: Banner of Truth, 1974), 2:557; emphasis mine.
3. Augustine, *Confessions*, bk. 10, chap. 31.

Chapter 5: Divine Power and Precious Promises

1. Milton Vincent, *A Gospel Primer for Christians: Learning to See the Glories of God's Love* (Bemidji, MN: Focus, 2008), 31–32.

Chapter 6: The Bread of Life and Bagels for Breakfast

1. Richard Sibbes, *The Tender Heart* (Carlisle, PA: Banner of Truth, 2000), 41–42.

Chapter 7: All Grace and All Sufficiency

1. D. A. Carson, *A Call to Spiritual Reformation: Priorities from Paul and His Prayers* (Grand Rapids, MI: Baker, 1992), 58.

Chapter 8: He Washes Us White as Snow

1. Julia Johnston, "Grace Greater Than Our Sin," 1911.
2. William Cowper, "There Is a Fountain," 1772.
3. Robert Lowry, "Nothing but the Blood," 1876.
4. John Ensor, *The Great Work of the Gospel: How We Experience God's Grace* (Wheaton, IL: Crossway, 2006), 110.

Chapter 9: God's Abiding Presence in Our Pain

1. Martin Luther, quoted in *Luther: Letters of Spiritual Counsel*, trans. and ed. Theodore G. Tappert, (Vancouver, BC: Regent College, 2003), 54.
2. Bryan Chappell, *Praying Backwards: Transform Your Prayer Life by Beginning in Jesus' Name* (Ada, MI: Baker, 2005).

Chapter 10: United with Christ but Lonely for Friends

1. Deepak Raju, Biblical Counseling Training, Redeemer Church of Dubai, Dubai, United Arab Emirates, January 2012.
2. Milton Vincent, *A Gospel Primer for Christians: Learning to See the Glories of God's Love* (Bemidji, MN: Focus, 2008), 29.

Chapter 13: Does Contentment in Christ Come with a Nap?

1. Jeremiah Burroughs, *The Rare Jewel of Christian Contentment* (Carlisle, PA: Banner of Truth, 1964), 18–19.
2. Ibid.
3. Burroughs, *Rare Jewel*, 219.
4. For a book that deals thoroughly and biblically with this issue see Staci Eastin's *The Organized Heart*, which is a gospel-centered approach to dealing with the idols in a woman's heart. *The Organized Heart: A Woman's Guide to Conquering Chaos* (Adelphi, MD: Cruciform, 2011).

General Index

Scripture Index